TELLING
THE
SEASONS

STORIES,
CELEBRATIONS
AND FOLKLORE
AROUND
THE YEAR

TELLING
THE
SEASONS

STORIES,
CELEBRATIONS
AND FOLKLORE
AROUND
THE YEAR

MARTIN MAUDSLEY

ILLUSTRATED BY ALISON LEGG

The
History
Press

For Ruth,
the one who makes the fun happen.

Special thanks to Matthew Pennington for the recipes in this book.

First published 2022

Reprinted 2023

The History Press
97 St George's Place, Cheltenham,
Gloucestershire, GL50 3QB
www.thehistorypress.co.uk

British Library Cataloguing in Publication Data.
A catalogue record for this book is available from the British Library.

ISBN 978 0 7509 9671 6

Typesetting and origination by The History Press
Printed and bound in Great Britain by TJ Books Limited, Padstow, Cornwall.

Trees for LYfe

Contents

Foreword

The seasons are part of all of our lives, our language and our culture. Seasonality is experienced in all places, rural and urban alike, binding us to nature and the passing of time. As a nation we have been fascinated with measuring and predicting daily and seasonal change, with sundials, weather kites, barometers and tide bells all invented to help people navigate daily life and foretell what the skies and tides will bring tomorrow. The seasons are part of us, embedded in the joy we feel when spring comes or the blues we feel in midwinter. Our culture and language are bristling with music, art, poems, sayings, metaphors and stories, all binding our feelings and thoughts to nature and the seasons. Red sky at night, clear moon frost soon. We can feel 'right as rain', have 'sunny dispositions' or feel 'foggy' in the morning. Some of us are 'night owls', some may prefer to 'wake with the lark', some are glad to be 'mad as a March hare'.

Our deep relationship with nature and the cycle of the seasons has long been celebrated by communities in every corner of the country. May Day, Plough Sunday, Michaelmas, Lady Day, Twelfth Night; these were so important that they were fixtures in the cultural calendar, expressing a community's reliance on nature and a need to celebrate together. Today, it may seem as if only a few of these seasonal celebrations have survived – Halloween, Christmas – but barely discernible under their commercial gloss. But beneath the surface of mainstream culture, in the nooks and cracks, there is a growing resurgence in communal celebration, a bursting of expression that resists the general trends of homogenisation in twenty-first century life. We may no longer be bound by harvest and husbandry to the cycle of the seasons, yet thankfully we cannot stop ourselves noticing the shifting seasons, telling our friends and neighbours about seeing the first snowdrops or bluebells, sharing news of the first returning swift or swallow. This need to share what we notice, to celebrate place and the passage of time, is deep-rooted. And stories have always been our most primal and essential way of sharing our experiences of the world. From parent to child, across communities, from one generation to the next, seasonal stories travel around and become important landmarks in an anxious, changing world.

For several years, Martin Maudsley has been a storyteller-in-residence for Common Ground, helping us demonstrate – from Dorset and Devon, to Manchester and Yorkshire – how seasonality can inspire new attitudes to understanding, while celebrating locality. In these pages, as he weaves old stories with new times, you'll find the most sumptuous and beautiful gleanings of his rich life as an ecological storyteller, and enjoy each tale as it resonates through time and place. But don't just keep them to yourself. These story-gifts are generous, and always have been. They do not belong to any one person or community. They are not fixed to a particular place. They are dynamic, borrowed, adapted, passed on. They are an offering for you to share too. Take them into your home, into your school or community, and use them to revive old celebrations or start new ones. Why not start an annual Apple Day celebration, a cake month, bluebell picnics, a full-moon walking club or a society of swift-nest mappers? Because celebrating your local wildlife and landscapes is the root of meaningful conservation, and bringing people together strengthens community resilience and cohesion through uncertain times.

Adrian Cooper, Executive Director of Common Ground

Acknowledgements

The process of gathering ideas and stories for *Telling the Seasons* stretches back over a period of twenty years as a professional storyteller, with many fellow storytellers (more than I can mention individually) kindly contributing along the way. A particular thank you to word-weaver Jane Flood, whose gentle wisdom infuses both her own storytelling and our long-standing friendship. I'm grateful also to Kevan Manwaring who took the time to read through and comment on the manuscript. A special mention also to Ian Siddons Heginworth, whose wonderful book – *Environmental Therapy and the Tree of Life* – has been a creative inspiration and constant companion in my own reflective journeys through the cycle of the seasons.

Tom Munro and his team at Dorset AONB provided many opportunities (and welcome financial support!) for storytelling projects and seasonal events that have helped to shape my thinking about the book's content. I'm also grateful to Darren Moore at the Woodman Inn – a proper community pub – for hosting regular spoken word and folk music events that celebrate the seasons, including outings of Bridport Mummers' Society (who are always well 'paid' in liquid assets). Jon Woolcott and Gracie Cooper from Little Toller Books kindly offered useful insights into the business of writing, during shared Tuesdays working in their fantastic little bookshop in Beaminster. I'm especially grateful to Adrian Cooper, editor at Little Toller and executive director of Common Ground, for reading early drafts, contributing the book's foreword and all his generous advice and encouragement in writing about seasonal celebrations over the years. In my role as storyteller-in-residence at Common Ground, I'm pleased, and proud, to have been part of a long-term project in Manchester with Jane Doyle and Freya Morton, telling and recording stories around the wheel of the year. Many of the seasonal folk tales in the book were first told within a Forest School setting, with a wonderfully 'wild' group of children from St Mary's Levenshulme RC Primary.

I'm extremely grateful for the hard work and artistic talent of Alison Legg in creating the wealth of original drawings within the text. It's not an easy task to capture the essence of the written content, but her illustrations of plants, animals and cultural traditions are beautifully sensitive to the seasonal shifts in time. Similarly, Matthew Pennington has gone well beyond the bounds of duty in creating original recipes for each month. Drawing on both his passion for cooking and deep knowledge of wild food, he has generously spent many hours researching, testing and tasting, for which I am deeply indebted.

The main writing period of the book coincided with the Covid-19 pandemic and several lockdowns – not to mention periods of 'writer's block'. For helping to keep my head above the water in tricky times, I'm deeply grateful to my family and Bridport friends, including Dickie, Nick and Nathan, plus all the denizens of 'Sadness Copse'. Most of all, my partner Ruth Mackay provided epic levels of support and legendary amounts of patience during the whole writing period. Also, huge hugs to my two amazing children Orran and Annie, who have listened to me telling stories many times. I've relished all our wild adventures through the seasons as a family – here's to many more!

Introduction

The Wheel of the Year

'There's time ... and there's time,' as storyteller Hugh Lupton once said. 'Time that travels forward in a straight line, and time that travels round in circles.'*

This book is about circular time: the cycle of the seasons around the wheel of the year. It draws on folk tales and folklore, celebrations and customs, that together hold our shared experiences and cultural expressions of the turning seasons. Although many such traditions stretch back in time, accrued over past generations, they continue to offer insights and inspiration for us to connect with the recurring rhythms of nature. Our innate desire to gather together socially is also fulfilled through the auspices of the seasons: from midwinter feasts to midsummer fires; from May Day to Apple Day. Seasonal celebrations help us to navigate the year, through personal connections and communal interactions, engendering a deep-rooted sense of both time and place. There are many powerful reasons why we're impelled to celebrate the seasons, but I'm reminded of a fable in fellow storyteller Peter Stevenson's book, *Welsh Folk Tales*, briefly retold in my own words:

> One springing morning a skylark rose up on her ladder of song above a little orchard where an old pig was tied to a tree. The boar looked up with small, squinting eyes and grunted loudly at the frivolous bird: 'Why do you fly so high and sing so loudly, when no-one gives a fig for your song?' The skylark replied: 'I sing because it's spring and the sun is shining, and because unlike you I'm not tethered to a tree.'

---

* Paraphrased from *Christmas Champions*, a musical storytelling show with folk singer Chris Wood about mummers' plays. Hearing it was a personal inspiration in terms of both story-telling and seasonal celebrations.

The Wheel of The Year

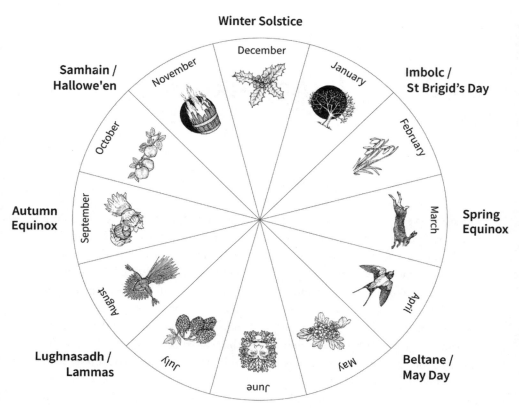

Winter Solstice

Samhain /
Hallowe'en

Imbolc /
St Brigid's Day

November

December

January

October

February

Autumn
Equinox

September

March

Spring
Equinox

August

April

Lughnasadh /
Lammas

July

May

Beltane /
May Day

June

Summer Solstice

The word calendar derives from the Latin verb *calare*, meaning to 'call out', in reference to vocal acknowledgement of seeing the new moon each month from Roman times. Like skylarks, we have been merrily singing the seasons and calling out auspicious times of year since the dawn of humanity. The custom calendar in Britain and Ireland therefore comprises a rich mix of many cultural influences; underpinned by physical factors such as astronomy, climate and geography. In structuring the monthly chapters of this book, I have highlighted three main spokes in the festive wheel of the year: the stations of the sun as marked in the old Celtic calendar; the evocative Anglo-Saxon namings for months and full moons; and the parade of annual saints' feast days through the Christian church's liturgical year. Some prominent Roman rituals and festivals are also included, especially where they help illuminate the origins of familiar seasonal customs.

The Silver Apples of the Moon, the Golden Apples of the Sun

I talk with the moon, said the owl
While she lingers over my tree,
I talk with the moon, said the owl
And the night belongs to me.

I talk with the sun, said the wren
As soon as he starts to shine,
I talk with the sun, said the wren
And the day is mine.

In the Northern Hemisphere, the solar year is intrinsically divided into four equal quarters by the seasonal summits of winter and summer solstices (when daylight is at its lowest and highest) and the midpoints of spring and autumn equinoxes (when day and night are equal length). The specific dates vary slightly from year to year, but fall around the twenty-first day of the month in December, March, June and September, in succession. In the pre-Christian Celtic calendar, the year was sub-divided into eighths through four additional celebrations that herald the inception of each season: Imbolc (1st February) for spring, Beltane (1st May) for summer, Lammas (1st August) for autumn and Samhain for winter (1st November). The festivities generally began the night before, with the lighting of flames outdoors, and are often referred to as the four fire festivals, or sometimes as cross-quarter days. These moments of seasonal transition were particularly luminous, and numinous, in our ancestral past: ripe with superstition and in rich myths and legends, that continue to reverberate into modern times.

These markers might seem slightly out of phase with conventional meteorological definitions of the four seasons. However, they chime in tune with much of the farming traditions and seasonal folklore of Britain and Ireland, as well as with natural cycles. For example: there are many visible stirrings in the wild world by the beginning of February, from flowers to frogspawn, long before many people would declare for spring in mid-March. Alongside Celtic festivals based on the solar year, the Anglo-Saxon lunar almanac offers many descriptive insights into how we have adapted culturally and agriculturally to the seasons. Their traditional names for monthly full moons are particularly resonant, such as the widely recognised Harvest Moon, occurring closest to the autumn equinox in September. Others are less familiar now, such as Milk Moon in May or Hay Moon in July, but are equally vivid as seasonal descriptors in the climate and landscapes of these islands. It should be noted that the named full moons can vary slightly in which month they fall, due to discrepancies between lunar and solar cycles – they are realigned each year at spring and autumn equinoxes. There are also many Old English or Germanic names for the calendar months themselves that help highlight connections between people, place and time of year. These are often quite matter-of-fact and relatable in modern times, as in the designation of 'mud month' for February!

When the Saints go Marching in

The church calendar comprises a rich tapestry of high days and holidays that once offered many other occasions for social interactions and seasonal merry-making through the year, particularly in medieval England. Some of the festivals of Christian saints were adopted and assimilated from earlier, pagan celebrations (e.g. Imbolc developing into St Brigid's Day). Others simply gathered their own folk traditions over time (e.g. Michaelmas), helping to add resonance and relevance for those living in close connection to the land and the seasons. The original interpretation of the Latin *paganus* simply referred to a 'country dweller', so it's likely that some Christian rituals were gradually 'paganised' through the everyday practices of rural people. With one or two exceptions, such as St Valentine's Day perhaps, few of the saints' days are widely or loudly celebrated anymore. However, they continue to provide meaningful markers through the year for folklore, food and festivities; and perhaps are ripe for renewal. The Church calendar also prescribed the four 'quarter days' that evenly divide the year, and once held huge importance in regulating agricultural practices, commercial arrangements and seasonal fairs. In England these were: Lady Day (25th March), Midsummer's Day (23rd June), Michaelmas Day (29th September) and Christmas Day (25th December). Again, these dates are clearly closely aligned with older seasonal celebrations of the solstices and equinoxes.

Keeping Up with Tradition

Tradition is not the worship of ashes but keeping the flames alive.

Gustav Mahler

In many ways, this book is a collection of traditions: traditional tales, customs and celebrations. But use of the adjective 'traditional' should not be taken as being synonymous with old-fashioned, out-dated or behind the times. From its Latin roots, the word 'tradition' comprises two elements: *trans* (meaning 'across') and *dare* (meaning 'to give'). Thus, its intended meaning could be expressed as 'to give across' or 'hand over'. Tradition, therefore, refers to a mode of transmission: the passing on of stories, skills, information or ideas, by word of mouth, from person to person, across generations. As well as carrying an inherent sense of generosity, it's also open-ended. Traditions survive, or are revived, because they still carry meaning and are valued within communities where they take place. Although rooted in history, many of the seasonal celebrations and customs highlighted within this book can be seen as living traditions, rather than traditional beliefs.

The prefix 'trans-' also relates to 'change', and there's an implicit understanding that as traditions are passed on, they are free to change in the hands of the next person. There's no compulsion to do things exactly as they've always been, yet they provide a helpful, familiar framework to start from, before weaving in new strands and associations. Traditional music sometimes shares the same sentiments, as folk singer Chris Wood once commented, 'Tradition should be respected, convention should be broken.' As well as being progressive, traditional customs are often highly non-conformist, subverting the norms of conventional living and breaking the routines of everyday life. What could be more radical than climbing a hill in the dark on a May morning to greet the sun, or standing in a cold orchard to toast the naked apple trees in January? Such seasonal traditions are inherently wild and playful in nature; but a glass of ale or drop of cider always seem to help participants revel in the occasion.

Well-Seasoned Stories

> The question we should ask of myth is not is it true or false, but whether it carries meaning in our time.
>
> *R. Holloway, quoted in Richard Mabey's* The Cabaret of Plants

It's unsurprising, given our long-standing and dependent relationship with the changing seasons, that they are deeply woven within the stories we've told each other over time. Folk tales, and folklore, offer both a window into past intimacies and also an abiding means of making sense of the world around us, with all its shifting seasonal subtleties. Each chapter of this book, from January to December, begins with a 'framing' story to set the seasonal scene for that particular month. These are retellings of traditional tales, mostly British and Irish; many of which I've told in person at seasonal events through the year. A few more folk tales are scattered through the pages to illustrate and illuminate the magic and mystery of each monthly moment. I've included one or two myths from other northern European countries that hold specific, unique symbolism of the seasons (e.g. Dawn and Dusk, an Estonian folk tale retold in June).

Folk tales often have their seasonal significance in terms of indicative plants and animals, from precocious snowdrops to springing hares and summer moths to autumn foxes. Several of the seasonal stories feature 'shape-shifting': the supernatural ability for humans to transform into animals or trees, and vice versa – perhaps highlighting our close relationship, biologically and culturally, with the rest of the natural world. Therefore, each chapter includes a few salient references to wild sightings and sounds for that month; that help us to 'tell the season'. Geographical location clearly plays an important role in seasonal phenomena, such as the arrival of migrant birds and the timing of wild harvests. I freely, and happily, admit that my own observations and perceptions are biased towards south-west England, where I have lived and worked for many years. Within each chapter there are also several well-observed and finely drawn illustrations by Dorset artist Alison Legg. Like flowers pressed between the pages, they complement the stories and help conjure the imagery of the natural world through the changing seasons.

The capriciousness of nature, as well as the boom or bust nature of living from the land, are often vividly brought to life through traditional tales about the fairy folk. They are quick to anger and fickle in their affections, yet capable of unexpected and unbridled acts of generosity. Such 'fairy tales' seem to flourish at specific, seasonally sensitive times of year, in particular the start of summer (May), harvest time (August) and the onset of winter (November). Stories of the Good Neighbours remind us to keep, or restore, the covenant of customs between ourselves and the unseen forces that regulate the natural world. Several stories also feature examples of 'folk magic' – repeated rituals that make sense of, and hopefully mitigate, the unpredictability of the seasons and the vagaries of the weather (and/or the fairies). Perhaps, the underlying principles in such practices still ring true: being grateful for what we've got, satisfied with enough and remaining hopeful for the future.

A Taste of the Seasons

There's nothing quite like food, glorious food for creating a sense of festivity and marking a moment in the cycle of the seasons. As well as a liberal sprinkling of food-related folklore throughout the book, there is also a bespoke recipe for each month – created by Matthew Pennington, owner/chef at the Ethicurean restaurant in Wrington, near Bristol. I've been lucky to work alongside the restaurant for many years at festive events, notably their annual winter wassail – a wild and well-fed affair. Around the year, they produce changing menus of fresh, local, seasonal, ethical, and above all delicious, food. No one pays more attention to when, where and how food is sourced and served. Under the heading of Flavour of the Month, Matthew offers twelve food and drink ideas; each tailored to the ingredients and inspiration of the season. The recipes are miniature stories in themselves; weaving together culinary traditions, foraged flavours and innovative techniques.

Old Roots, New Shoots

This book is not a comprehensive compendium of the whole calendar of British and Irish festivities – a gloriously bountiful and wide-ranging topic, and covered by a great many other volumes. Instead, the focus here is on celebrations and traditions that directly relate to aspects of seasonal phenomena in the outdoor world, both wild and cultivated. Also, as a storyteller, I have been drawn to celebrations with a strong narrative element, either in their origins or how they relate to existing myths and legends.

Since 2015 I've been storyteller-in-residence at Common Ground, a groundbreaking environmental arts charity based in Dorset. For many years, they have been at the forefront of championing both natural diversity and local distinctiveness through shared cultural expression. In the 1990s, under the inspired leadership of Sue Clifford and Angela King, Common Ground successfully established two brand new seasonal celebrations in the UK: Apple Day (in October) and Tree Dressing Day (in December). In doing this they incorporated wide-ranging traditions and current environmental concerns, whilst bringing new vigour to the festive calendar. Since then, there has been a conspicuous surge in the prevalence and popularity of revived or reinvented seasonal celebrations, from blossom festivals to winter wassails, and many others around the year. These locally expressed festivities foster tangible connections between people, place and time of year; whilst avoiding overtly religious, commercial or political affiliations.

Fuelled by this spirit of revival, and drawing on the ethos and innovation of Common Ground, the potential for recreating further seasonal celebrations are ripe and rife. Crucially these could, and should, feature a diverse range of seasonal highlights that resonate most strongly within different local communities. For instance: celebrating the return of swifts in late spring; revelling in the floweriness of a local hay meadow in high summer; and savouring the fruits or changing leaves of a local, landmark tree in autumn. It's also an opportunity to draw deep from the well of local history, initiating an annual occasion for telling the tales of positive parochial characters that have helped to shape the nature of the local area. At the end of each chapter there is a short section, 'Old Roots, New Shoots', exploring some of these ideas, drawing freely on the cultural traditions and natural wonders of each month, with suggestions for new expressions. Hopefully, some scattered seeds will find fertile ground, widening and diversifying our calendar of seasonal celebrations yet further in years to come.

Changing Times

In the UK, and most of the western world, the year is chronologically organised according to the Gregorian calendar. The previous system, the Julian Calendar, failed to accurately account for the orbit of the Earth around the sun, and over time was slowly slipping out of phase. Many Catholic countries on the European continent were early adopters of the calendrical shift, but Britain didn't accept the substitution until the Calendar (New Style) Act of 1750. The actual change took place in 1752: when 2nd September was followed by 14th September, overnight (losing 11 days). Although it was made law to adhere to the revised dates, the new style calendar was greeted with both confusion and resentment of time-honoured traditions being desecrated by the authorities. To this day, several seasonal celebrations still follow the Old Calendar – such as Old Twelfth Night for wassailing.

Such slips in time may have caused an uproar in their day, but on the whole annual celebrations more or less kept in touch with the seasons. More recent, man-made climatic shifts, however, are causing much more widespread, disruptive and worrying effects. The changing seasons themselves are now in a state of flux. Most notable in Britain and Ireland, perhaps, is the increasingly early arrival of spring. Phenology – the scientific study of natural phenomena – has documented a whole string of precocious arrivals, openings and behaviours. Recent evidence suggests that many spring 'events' now happen a whole month earlier than they did just forty years ago.

Sadly, and ironically, there are now several seasonal festivities that have become dislocated from their underlying cause for celebration: for instance, Cuckoo Fairs in April often take place without an appearance of their star attraction. On the other hand, continuing to intentionally mark the passing of the seasons through the year allows opportunity to regularly (re)connect with the natural world around us. Witnessing changes for ourselves, first-hand and in our own particular patch, can be the first step in caring, and then sharing, about what is happening in the wider wild world. What's more, allowing ourselves to pay attention to circular, perennial time can engender a sense of reciprocity and self-restraint – the need to give back, in order to take out. Similarly, many traditional tales hold both stark warnings of the consequences of breaking natural constraints but also the redemptive possibilities of emotional and practical change. Finally, there is much inherent joyfulness in being an active part of local seasonal celebrations – it invigorates the spirit and defies despondency. 'There's a worse crime than crass destruction, and that's crass despair,' wrote Simon Barnes in *How to be a Bad Birdwatcher*. Celebrating the cycle of the seasons around the wheel of the year, outdoors and in good company, is the best antidote to despair of which I know.

Martin Maudsley
Candlemas, 2022

1

January

We know by the moon we are not too soon,
We know by the sky we are not too high,
We know by the stars we are not too far,
We know by the ground that we are within sound.

The Twelve Months

Once there was a girl called Mary, who lived in a cottage at the edge of a forest. As she grew up, she brought great joy to both her parents: bright as spring, soft as summer and honest as autumn. But, one cold, cruel winter, her mother became ill and quickly died. Not long after, her father married again; believing his daughter needed a feminine presence at home. However, his new wife arrived with her own daughter and barely concealed contempt towards Mary. Whilst her father was working in the woods, the stepmother forced Mary to do all the housework, as well as feeding the chickens and milking the cow. The days were long and hard for Mary but, being sweet natured, she did all that was demanded of her, without mentioning anything to her father.

One January day, as cold northerly winds brought heavy falls of snow, her father had to go into town for a week. Poor Mary was left alone with her stepmother and stepsister, who gleefully saw an opportunity to be rid of Mary for once and all.

The next morning the stepmother came into the kitchen and said, 'Mary, go into the forest and pick primroses. I want to see their bright yellow petals shining in my daughter's hair.'

'How could I do such a thing?' replied Mary. 'Primroses don't grow in the snow!'

'Do as I say, or your father will hear how horrible and rude you are!'

Unwilling to disappoint her father, Mary wrapped her thin woollen shawl around her shoulders and stepped outside into the cold. She had no idea where to go, so headed north into the white, winter weather. She walked until the snow slid down her boots, numbing her toes, and her face was pinched with icy cold. Eventually, she came to the forest and there, between the bare birches, was a flickering fire. Edging closer, she saw a circle of twelve men and women sitting round the fire; all different ages and all dressed differently. On the highest seat was an old woman wrapped in a wolf-skin cloak with flowing, snowy-white hair and skin as fair as frost. Her eyes glinted bright blue in the firelight. Mary was utterly amazed by what she saw, but feeling suddenly colder, she stepped forward and politely addressed the old woman: 'Grandmother, please may I warm myself by your fire?'

The old crone smiled at Mary and beckoned her to come closer. 'My name is Mother January. These are my brothers and sisters: together we are the Twelve Months. But what brings you to these woods on a cold winter's day?'

Mary told her story, explaining that she needed to somehow find primroses to take back to her stepmother. Old Mother January shook her head sadly, but then stood up and walked over to one of the men in the circle. He was much younger than her – as slender as a willow sapling, with smooth skin and bright, green eyes. 'Brother March, please take my place for a while,' she said.

March swapped positions with Mother January. With his own ash wood wand, he started to stir the flames, which blazed bright green. Immediately, the snow melted, the birch trees burst into leaf and the ground was carpeted with pale yellow primroses beneath the trees. 'Pick them quickly!' said March, his voice lilting like birdsong.

As quickly as she could, Mary gathered a posy of primroses then, thanking Mother January and Brother March, she scampered home as fast as she could across the snow. When she opened the door, her stepsister and stepmother looked up with undisguised surprise – they'd assumed she was already frozen to death in the snow. But they took the flowers to arrange in their hair, and ordered Mary to get on with her chores.

Early next morning, as Mary was laying the fire, the stepmother came into the kitchen and said, 'Mary, we've decided that we want something sweet to eat for breakfast. Go and bring back ripe strawberries from the forest.'

'What? Strawberries don't grow in the snow!'

But the stepmother angrily grabbed Mary by the arm and pushed her out of the door, before she'd even had chance to put on her shawl. At least Mary knew the way: she walked through the snow and into the forest of birch trees, until she saw the flickering fire. Old Mother January was once more sitting at the head of the Circle of Seasons, stirring the flames. Mary stepped forward and bowed respectfully as she told of her task to find strawberries. Mother January smiled kindly, then approached the woman sitting exactly opposite her in the circle. 'Sister June, please take my place for a while.'

Sister June was wearing a leafy gown of many different shades of green with a wreath of roses crowning her lustrous, golden hair. She readily swapped places with January, then began to stir the fire with an oaken wand. Instantly the flames leapt higher; yellow and orange, as bright as the sun itself. The snow suddenly melted and the trees were green again; small birds singing in their branches. Mary watched in wonder as underneath the trees, green plants with white blossoms started to produce ripe, red berries. 'Pick them quickly!' said June, warmly.

Mary picked the strawberries, popping a few in her mouth, but soon filling her wicker basket. Thanking both Mother January and Sister June, she ran home swiftly, still savouring the flavour of the strawberries. Her stepmother and stepsister were even more surprised to see Mary back this time – although their dismay soon turned to delight when they tasted the juicy strawberries, which they gobbled greedily until their chins were stained red.

Having enjoyed the sweet strawberries, the very next day the stepmother demanded Mary go back into the forest to bring a basket of ripe apples. Wearily, Mary left the house and set out into the cold. Once more she walked, through snow and forest, to the clearing where the Twelve Months were sitting round their fire. Mother January welcomed Mary. Then, after hearing of her new plight, addressed one of the older men in the circle. 'Brother October, please take my place for a while.'

October was hale and hearty, dressed in brown deer-skins, his russet-red beard flecked with grey. He swapped seats with Mother January and stirred the fire with his apple wood wand, turning the flames a deep, crimson red. The snow melted away and the birch trees were again covered with leaves; not green but gold. Among the birches stood a solitary apple tree, its shiny red fruit hanging heavy on brown-leaved branches.

'Shake the tree!' said Brother October with a bristly grin. Willingly, Mary shook the tree and gathered the apples as they fell gently to the ground. She thanked Mother January and Brother October and ran home across the snow. This time the stepsister and the stepmother were waiting. They snatched the basket of apples and began to eat them immediately, biting through the thin skin and savouring the juicy flesh within. They'd never tasted anything so delicious and desirable in all their life. They looked at each other with greed glinting in their eyes.

'If this miserable wretch can find winter fruits, just think what we could fetch from the forest. We'll bring back bright treasures to live a life of luxury and leave Mary and her pathetic father to their own poverty.'

Wearing thick, fur coats and warm, leather boots, they set out into the wintry weather, following Mary's footsteps through the snow and into the wild woods. There they wandered around for a while, getting colder and angrier, until eventually they found the clearing with the Twelve Months sitting around the fire. Without asking permission, they rudely burst into the circle to warm themselves in front of its flames.

'What are you looking for?' asked Mother January, her blue eyes flashing.

'Give us diamonds and pearls, old hag!' they shouted, rudely.

Then Old Mother January shook her snowy white hair and began to stir the fire vigorously with her rowan wand – the flames turning bright blue. An icy wind blew through the trees and a flurry of fat snowflakes began to fall; as thickly as feathers shaken from a pillow. By the time Mother January's cold snowstorm had finished, the stepmother and stepsister were frozen solid where they stood – their still-open eyes shining like diamonds and their icy skin as pale as pearls.

A few days later, Mary's beloved father came back. He hugged his daughter warmly then listened, with both sadness and astonishment, to the cold tale she told. Mary never saw the Twelve Months again, although she often thought of them sitting round their fire in the forest. She loved all the changing seasons, but her favourite time of the year was January; the first and oldest of all the months.

Out with the Old, in with the New

The Old Year now away is fled,
The New Year now is entered ...

January, the first month of the year, takes its name from the Roman deity Janus – a god of beginnings and endings. He is typically portrayed with two faces, looking forwards and backwards at the same time. Literally translated, the Latin word *janua* refers to an arched gateway; as in the word janitor, meaning 'keeper of the gate'. The start of any new enterprise is considered to be fraught with danger and uncertainty (like Mary setting out to gather flowers in the snow). Therefore, the beginning of the year, the starting point of the cycle of the seasons, is suffused with superstitions and customs to avert ill fate and invite good fortune. After midnight on New Year's Eve, it is auspicious to open the back door before the front – letting the old year and its past problems out, before inviting the new one in. Similar folklore suggests that something should be taken out of the house on this day, before anything new is brought in:

Take out, take in,
Bad luck is sure to begin.
Take in, take out,
Good luck will come about.

Exchanging gifts is an ancient custom at New Year, pre-dating Christmas and stretching back to Roman times. Thresholds are again symbolically important, as guests bearing offerings step through the doorways of neighbouring houses on New Year's Eve, in a custom known as first-footing – still common in Scotland and parts of northern England. Favoured items, varying with locality, include coal, bread, fish and whisky. In the past, it was traditional for tenant farmers to also give presents of food, typically poultry, to their landlords at this time. In Scotland, and nowadays many other places, the singing of Robert Burns's poem 'Auld Lang Syne' ('for old times' sake') bids farewell to the Old Year at the striking of the midnight bells on New Year's Eve. Fittingly, the birth of Scotland's much-loved bard is also celebrated at the end of this month, on Burns Night (25th January).

Old Flames

It's considered good luck to keep the hearth fires continually burning through the night on New Year's Eve, and traditionally farmers in Scotland burned juniper branches to ward away malign influences. Puritanical reactions against 'Catholic' Christmas meant that New Year gained greater prominence in Britain, and continues to hold pre-eminence in Scotland – as Hogmanay. Communal celebrations of New Year are often held outdoors with bonfires, burning torches and fireworks. A bright example is the Norse-infused Up Helly Aa festival in Lerwick on Shetland, which culminates in the enthusiastic burning of an entire wooden Viking ship. The annual Burning the Clavie celebration in Burghhead is held on 11th January, Old New Year's Eve – where a half barrel on a pole, filled with burning wood and tar, is processed sun-wise through the town. At various points around the town burnt embers are offered to pubs and prominent houses for good luck for the year ahead, similar to first-footing traditions.

Cold Moon Rising

The Man in the Moon a new light on us throws;
He's a man we all talk of but nobody knows.

The first new moon of the new year is rife with superstition, and traditionally should not be seen through glass; which could filter out the good fortune it otherwise brings. It's a good time to make a wish, or show your money to the moon (especially silver) – as the moon waxes, so your wealth will increase. One of the Anglo-Saxon designations for a full moon in January is Snow Moon, reflecting the likelihood of snowfall at this time of year. In Germanic mythology, winter snow was believed to be caused by a character called Frau Holle (also known as Old Mother Frost) as she shakes the feathers from her pillows; echoing Old Mother January in the Twelve Months story. Another Old English full moon name is Wolf Moon as they were often heard howling during winter months; although in Britain they have long since fallen silent.

Other forms of wildlife, however, can be seen and heard near to human habitation during the frosty days and cold moons of January. In particular, migrant thrushes are regular winter guests: redwings find refuge in the garden and larger fieldfares feast on fallen apples in the orchard. Similarly, resident birds, notably blackbirds and song thrushes, are often increasingly active and vocal in January, heralding the beginning the seasonal cycle of song in the natural world, which will slowly swell through the following months.

Twelfth Night

In the church calendar, Twelfth Night falls on 5th January, the eve of Epiphany – when the wise men presented their gifts to the infant Jesus. It also marks the end of festivities for the twelve days of Christmas, although in some traditions there's an extra day's grace, with 6th January designated as Twelfth

Night. Either way, work and domestic routines have generally replaced revelry by this date, leaving it only as the dreary deadline for taking the decorations down. In the past, however, it was enthusiastically enjoyed as a second bite of the cherry for agricultural workers whose main opportunity for merrymaking was the midwinter break. There was extra impetus for celebration, not to mention confusion, as the date for Christmas Day using the Old Calendar (see Introduction), was also 6th January. In the Middle Ages, it seems Twelfth Night reinvigorated seasonal festivities that often continued all the way to Candlemas on 2nd February – one way to beat the January blues!

Many culinary traditions became associated with Twelfth Night, including the making of festive cakes and seasonal drink of hot spiced ale served with roasted crab apples called Lamb's Wool (see this month's recipe). Several lively folk traditions were also tied to this date, such as Haxey Hood – a long-lived and much-loved seasonal affair between two competing villages in Lincolnshire. It's a colourful and complicated custom, often lasting all day, where up to 300 participants try to manoeuvre the 'hood', rugby scrum-style, into one of two opposing pubs. According to dubious local legend, the hood in question belonged to Lady de Mowbray, which was once blown off her head by a gust of winter wind, causing local labourers to fight between themselves to retrieve it for her. Perhaps the merriest of all Twelfth Night traditions is 'wassailing', in all its various revelrous forms, which crops up throughout the month, especially around 17th January – the date of Old Twelfth Night.

Flavour of the Month

Lamb's Wool

The origins of this recipe stretch back to the beginnings of the Ethicurean restaurant, when local cheese-makers Angela and Tim Homewood, ever faithful to the pagan year, reminded us that we had midwinter duties to the attached orchard. We decided to host our inaugural wassail, and threw everything into revealing the mystery and then revelling in the magic. After careful research, we created and cooked our version of Lamb's Wool, relishing its unusual, otherworldly flavour, as it led us into the dark, torchlit orchard.

Against a backdrop of the coldest nights of the year, this elixir is guaranteed to beat the doldrums. Although ancient, and somewhat muddled by time, it has a flavour that transcends the sum of its ingredients: dark, frothy and foreboding, yet also warm and nourishing. Whilst it's possible to make this recipe using farm cider, with dark porter or stout the flavour is more pronounced and intriguing against its white woollen froth.

Let's forgo a list of weighed ingredients here. For every bottle of dark ale, you'll need one medium, roasted cooking apple; cored and flesh pulped.

In your grandest pan, tickle the porter to a simmer with a stick of cassia or cinnamon, half a grated nutmeg and two whole star anise.

Stir in the roasted pulped apple and sweeten it lightly to taste with natural cane sugar.

Before pouring into tankards, it's customary to heavily whisk the brew, providing ample 'wool' for the cup from the roasted apple. The name Lamb's Wool undoubtedly derives from this distinctive part of the preparation.

Grate additional nutmeg atop each frothing mug – you'll need two servings per person, at least, to scare away the bad spirits on a frigid January night.

We're Wassailing

Wassail! Wassail! All over the town,
Our toast it is white and our ale it is brown.

The word wassail comes from an Old English phrase *waes hael*, literally meaning 'be healthy', as in hale and hearty. It originated in our Saxon-infused cultural past as a drinking salutation at midwinter feasts – a season when good cheer was both needed and relished. The traditional response to the toast was *drink hael*

– literally meaning 'drink healthy'; as in drink deep until you feel well, rather than any modern connotations of healthy moderation!

Later, in England in particular, it became a popular seasonal custom for labouring workers to visit prominent farms and manor houses to ask for food and drink in exchange for rough and ready entertainment; as in the mummers' plays and Mari Lwyd traditions (see December). At the end of the visitation, a toast would be proposed to the master and mistress of the household: wishing them prosperity for the year ahead. The word wassail is used freely as both noun and verb, and is also synonymous with the alcoholic beverage that is generously supplied in a shared bowl throughout the evening, such as Lamb's Wool or mulled cider. In western parts of Britain, where apples are widely grown and cider-making flourishes, wassailing became bound together with wishing good health to the orchard and raising a toast to the Apple Tree Man himself.

The Apple Tree Man

Once, in old Somerset, there was an old farmer, who loved the land where he lived and worked for his whole life. The farmer had two grown sons who, even though they were brothers, were as different as apples and pears. The oldest son was cheerful and charming, and cherished the farm like his father. The younger brother, on the other hand, was moody, miserable and mean-spirited. But, when their father died, it was the youngest son who, according to custom of those times, inherited the whole farm and his elder brother had to beg for a place to live.

'You can have that old shed on the hill,' said the younger brother. 'And the little apple orchard around it. You can even have the stable and any animals that are left alive inside. But you must pay me a rent: a silver sixpence, every year, on Twelfth Night.'

The elder brother couldn't argue against the law, so he went up the hill to see what he'd got. But the door of the shed fell off its hinges as he opened it, the windows were broken and there were big gaping holes in the roof. Inside the stable there were two pitiful, decrepit old creatures: a donkey with a stiff leg and an ox with a bent back. In the orchard, there were three apple trees, wizened with age, and one of the trees still had a single, red apple in its branches. But as he climbed the tree and picked the apple, it crumbled to dust in his fingers.

Feeling thoroughly dejected for the first time in his life, the elder brother suddenly remembered a piece of advice from his father: 'If you're ever in trouble, go and seek the help of the old hen-wife.' He set off at once, and soon arrived at a clearing in the nearby woods, where an old woman was bent over feeding her chickens.

'Good day, mother,' he called out. 'I need your help …'

The old woman looked him up and down, then replied: 'Come inside and let's talk …'

By the fire, inside her turf-roof hut, the wise woman listened carefully to the young man's story. She then asked if he had any money to pay the rent. 'Only one penny!' he replied.

'Well give that penny to me and in return I'll give you some good advice …'

After taking the money, she told him to start by taking good care of his animals. So she taught him how to forage for healing plants and make them into a medicine. At the end of the day, he thanked the old woman and returned home, gathering herbs along the way. Every day, from then on, he put a herbal poultice on the leg of the donkey and onto the back of the ox. Before long, they were both getting better: the donkey was walking freely and the back of the ox began to straighten and strengthen. What's more, the animals took to eating that medicinal mush as it fell to the ground, which filled them with vim and vigour. And as every farmer knows, what goes in must come out. Soon the elder brother was shovelling manure from the stable onto the roots of the old apple trees. By springtime, they were covered in blossom and by autumn the branches were weighed down with fruit. Some of the apples he ate, but most of them he turned into strong scrumpy cider, and for the rest of the year he had something good to drink. By the end of the year, the older brother was as healthy and hearty as his animals and the apple trees.

Christmas passed quietly, without much festivity, until on Twelfth Night there was a sudden knock at the door. There was his younger brother, standing on the doorstep: 'Happy New Year, brother! I've just come to remind you about the rent, which is due this very night …'

'Oh dear, I'd forgotten all about it!' said the eldest son, in sudden despair.

'Well, I'm sure we can come to an arrangement. I've been reading Father's old books, which tell of an ancient treasure buried somewhere on this farm. They also say that on Twelfth Night the animals on this farm have the power of speech – so they might talk about where that treasure is. So, here's the deal: let me listen to your animals in the stable tonight and I'll let you off your rent – just for one year.'

The eldest son now had no money at all, so once more he had to agree, and then he went inside and tipped up the cider barrel. But his luck was out – there was only half a glass left. He was just about to drink it, when he remembered the old custom that his father always followed at that time of year: toasting an orchard and wishing good health to the Apple Tree Man. A few moments later he was standing in the orchard, in front of the biggest, oldest tree. He raised his glass and spoke his father's words:

Apple tree, apple tree,
What you have given to me, I give back to you.
Grow well roots, bear well tops,
Next year may you bring a bumper apple crop!

Then he poured the half-glass of cider onto the tree's roots and was just about to turn away, when something strange happened. The tree started swaying from side to side, even though there was no wind in the air. Its branches became limbs, twigs turned into fingers and a wrinkled old face appeared within the bark of the trunk.

'Was that you?' said the Apple Tree Man. 'Oh, I do like a drop of my own juice and it's been a long time since anyone's given me any cider! Well, you've been good to me, and so I'll be good to you. Go and fetch a spade then dig underneath my big, left root – but don't tell your brother about whatever you find …'

Then, with a satisfied sigh, the Apple Tree Man turned back into a tree. The older brother grabbed a spade and carefully dug underneath the tree's roots. Sure enough, he uncovered an old metal box, filled with gold sovereigns, which he quickly hid beneath his bed. Not long later, the younger brother came up the hill and sat by the stable door to listen to the donkey and the ox. He waited and waited, until eventually the church clock stuck twelve. Then, the animals began to talk: they talked about their good health, they talked about how well the orchard was doing, they talked about the kindness of the eldest son. But they didn't talk about the buried treasure – because it wasn't buried anymore!

Old Apple Tree, We Wassail Thee

Oh, little apple tree, we have come to wassail thee,
Will you bring some fruits for me, when the season changes?

In the West Country, local farming communities gather together in the orchard at this time of year, not only to bring themselves good cheer, but to wassail the fruit trees in their winter dormancy. As a folk ritual, as well as a seasonal celebration, it serves to gratefully acknowledge the productivity of the land and propitiate Mother Nature for a good, plentiful crop next year. In recent times orchard wassails have become a growing tradition across the UK, partly due to campaigns by Common Ground (who initiated Apple Day, see October). Among the new shoots, a few locations have very old traditions, such as Carhampton in Somerset, which has held an annual wassail in its local orchard for the last 200 years. Unlike Christmas festivities, brought ever earlier into the season and mostly taking place indoors, these outdoor orchard wassails embrace the dark and cold of mid-January. They allow us to relish winter and reset our seasonal clocks, refreshed and ready for the cycle of the year ahead. One (rather exclusive) group in Dorset holds a naked wassail to fully realise the cathartic potential!

Although there's plenty of local distinctiveness around the country, most wassail ceremonies roughly adhere to the same tried-and-tested recipe. Firstly, a wassail queen (and sometimes a king) is chosen to lead the ceremony; traditionally by hiding a bean or coin inside an apple cake. The procession of wassailers then makes its way, with music and dance, to the biggest and oldest apple tree in the orchard, known as the Apple Tree Man. A well-known, and highly participative, element of wassailing is making a loud noise to scare away the bad spirits from the trees. This is done with raucous shouting, and by banging pots and pans and/or firing shotgun blanks – either at the beginning of the ceremony or at the end (or both!). In some places this is known as apple howling. The Wassail Queen then dunks pieces of toast into a large vessel of cider, called the wassail bowl or loving cup, and places them in the branches of the tree to feed the birds; especially robins, as spirits of good fortune. Then a generous dose of local cider is sprinkled onto the roots of the tree, to bring good health and fertility into the whole orchard for the year ahead. Finally, a toast (spoken or sung) is proposed to the tree, beseeching the orchard to produce a bumper apple crop at the next harvest.

Old apple tree, we wassail thee
And hoping thou will bear.

For who knows where we all shall be
At apples time this year.
For to grow well and to blow well
And merry all let us be.
Let everybody take off their hat
And sing to the old apple tree!

After the ceremony there's usually plenty of singing and storytelling around the fire, with a steady flow of cider, as the whole occasion mulls into merriness. There's a wealth of traditional wassailing songs, all with similar sentiments but varying melodies, usually named after their place of origin, e.g. Somerset wassail, Gower wassail, Cornish wassail etc.

The Night the Animals Talk

The Apple Tree Man story also highlights a time-honoured belief that farm animals gain the power of human speech on one day of the year during the festive season – either Christmas Eve or Twelfth Night. It's a tradition that is widespread in northern Europe with both pagan and Christian connections. In one version, God gives the animals voice in order to praise the miracle of Jesus's birth and, in a famous carol called 'The Friendly Beasts', the animals brag of their various roles in the Good News story. In darker seasonal folklore, however, it is said if you hear the animals talking, they tell only bad news; including the listener's own demise.

Ploughing On

Plough Monday is celebrated on the first Monday after Twelfth Night. Before the widespread cultivation of winter cereals, it marked the commencement of ploughing prior to spring sowing; therefore heralding the start of the arable agricultural year. In times past, a plough was an expensive and sought-after piece of equipment and often shared within rural communities. The day before is Plough Sunday, when the communal plough was dressed with colourful ribbons and blessed in the local church. After that it was proudly paraded through the streets by 'plough boys', who also took the opportunity to ask for donations for themselves – or else threaten to plough up the property of any unwilling landowners! Plough plays, a form of mummers' play (see December), continue to be performed on or around this date, particularly in the East Midlands. In Whittlesey, near Peterborough, an annual parade of distinctively costumed performers known as 'straw bears' takes place on, or just after, Plough Monday. In other locations, plough races provide a boisterous, competitive edge to getting ready for the farming year ahead.

An important ritualistic element of Plough Monday traditions is that of burying the corn dolly, made out of straw from the last cut of the cereal harvest (see August). As it holds the spirit of the corn, the dolly should be carefully returned to the earth in the first ploughed furrow, thus completing a full turn of the agricultural year. As one thing ends, so another begins. Reincarnation and renewal are richly recurring themes within seasonal folklore. And already the very first inklings of spring are stirring.

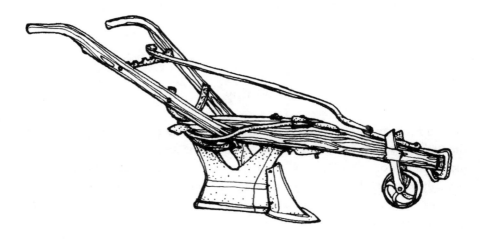

Old Roots, New Shoots

TELLING TALES

The dead of winter is when we need to believe the most: gathering together to tell tales, like the Twelve Months seated around the fire. Through shared narratives we encode our experiences, make sense of the world around us and imagine alternative realities. Traditional tales, honed over many generations of people, still speak loudly to the here and now – helping us to reconnect with each other and the natural world through all its seasons. Oral storytelling, as one of the world's oldest artforms, continues to flourish into modern times; its open-ended simplicity perhaps a welcome antithesis to highly pro-cessed mass media. The experience of storytelling – recreated in the moment, between teller and listener – is engaging, entertaining and sometimes deeply profound. Surely, it's something to be celebrated. So, since the year 2000, the end of January has marked the start of National Storytelling Week in England, organised by the Society for Storytelling. Hundreds of events now take place across the country every year in schools, theatres, care homes, pubs, village halls and out-doors – to celebrate the 'humanness' of stories. Once you've caught the storytelling bug, there are many annually recurring storytelling festivals across Britain and Ireland, that bring together storytellers from around the world to weave a tapestry of tales. So sit back, look into the flickering flames and let your imagination go wild …

2

February

Blessed Brigid comest thou in,
And bless this house and all within.

Bride Brings Spring

The Cailleach is the ancient Hag-Queen of Winter, as fierce as frost, who rules over the dark half of the year when the world is cold, stark and still. She dwells in the far north of Britain – the highlands of Scotland – where long ago she created the mountains by hurling huge boulders as she travelled around the countryside on a great, shaggy goat. The largest of those thrown-stone summits is Ben Nevis itself. Deep within that cold, craggy mountain, where winter never really ends, the Cailleach keeps her watch over the changing seasons. Every year in November, at the start of her wintry reign, she takes her pleated dresses and washes them in the sea – in the wild waters of the Corryvreckan whirlpool. Then, once they are sparkling clean and bleached bright white, she throws them over the tops of the mountains: as a covering of fresh, winter snow.

From time to time, over the years, the Cailleach would take young women from the nearby villages to be her servants; attending to all her demands and desires. One year, when the world was still young, she captured a beautiful maiden called Bride, whom she imprisoned in her mountain stronghold. In contrast to the Cailleach's frosty features and icy demeanour, Bride was warm and vibrant, with leaf-green eyes and a springing heart. Perhaps because of their contrasting differences, the Cailleach despised Bride and gave her ever more arduous chores, making her life a complete and utter misery. However, even within the cold confines of that mountain cave, Bride's bright spirit was undimmed. She bided her time through the dark times, waiting for a chance to escape the Cailleach's clutches.

One day, in the fierce frost of winter, the Cailleach gave Bride a dirty, brown fleece and ordered her to wash it in the waterfall behind the mountain, until it was as white as the snow. For days she persevered, frantically scrubbing the fleece, until her arms ached and her hands were red raw from the icy water. But even though the water turned filthy brown, the fleece refused to come clean. Eventually, after three long, despondent days, an old man quietly appeared by the side of the waterfall and asked what she was doing. On hearing Bride's desperate story, he nodded his head wisely, his pale blue eyes twinkling brightly beneath bushy, white brows.

'What's tainted by the Hag of Winter can only be made clean by the Old Man of Winter. Hand me the fleece and let's see what I can do ...'

Gratefully Bride passed him the fleece and watched, wide-eyed, as he shook it with three, quick flicks of his wrists. A shower of murky liquid arced through the air, leaving the woollen fleece as white and bright as freshly fallen snow. Bride thanked the old man, with tears of joy welling in her green eyes. But just as she was turning towards the mountain, he reached down amongst the snow and picked a posy of delicately drooping white flowers.

'Give these snowdrops to my sister, the Cailleach. If she asks where you found them, tell her the buds are about to burst in the forest and the greenery of spring is stirring beneath the snow!'

In hearing those warm words, and holding the freshly opened flowers in her hands, hope began to spring within Bride's heart. She ran back to the Cailleach's cave and laid the clean fleece at her feet. But the Cailleach was only interested in the white flowers that she held in her hand. 'Where did you get those?' she asked accusingly; eyes flashing, her words as sharp as daggers of ice.

'Beyond the waterfall,' Bride replied calmly. 'There the buds are ready to burst and green shoots are stirring beneath the snow.'

The Cailleach froze for a moment, then exploded into a ferocious fury. Her blustery cries reverberated against the walls of her mountain halls and echoed out across the winter sky, where there they thickened into thunder. Grabbing a huge, heavy cudgel, made from blackthorn wood, she jumped on her great, grey goat and rode off in a storm of anger. Wherever she rode across the country-side, beyond her mountain home, she brutally bludgeoned the emerging shoots with her blackthorn club and smashed the swelling buds from the branches.

The sounds of the Cailleach's tempestuous tantrum travelled far across many lands – even as far as the Green Isle in Tir na Nog, the Land of Youth. There they reached the ears of Angus Og, the youthful Lord of Summer, who lay sleeping and dreaming through winter on his warm bed of furs. Recently, however, his dreams had been filled with visions of a beautiful, green-eyed girl. In his febrile, fertile imagination Angus Og had seen Bride held captive by the Cailleach – his own mother – in her frozen fortress to the north. Now, awakened from his seasonal slumbers by the Cailleach's stormy cries and his own stirring desire, he was filled with determination to find Bride and set her free. He saddled his horse – a shimmering, milk-white mare – and rode swiftly over land and sea with long, golden hair and sun-yellow cape flying freely behind him. But the Cailleach saw his audacious flash of summer colours coming towards her. She regathered her stormy strength and roused all of her winter fury. Wild winds and showers of sleet, snow blizzards and stinging hail, battered and blew against poor Angus, preventing him from riding any closer to the mountains. For several days he battled bravely, urging his horse forward, but they couldn't match the ferocity of the Cailleach's witchety winter weather.

But then Angus Og, as one of the Cailleach's own offspring, drew deeply from his own elemental magic. Uttering an ancient incantation, he summoned forward three days from August; three days of gentle, generous weather. And in that brief spell of summer, he was able to still the storms – just long enough to reach the Cailleach's fortress. Bride, who'd witnessed from afar Angus' courageous contest against the wild elements, now seized her moment to escape. With surging strength flowing through her body, she broke free of the Cailleach's spells of confinement. Down from the mountainside she ran until she reached Angus Og, who pulled her up onto his horse and into his warm, welcoming embrace. Together they rode away from the Cailleach's cold realm and their newly growing affection was enough to inspire and infuse the quickening of spring wherever they went. Across the land, a blanket of white melted into a carpet of green, crowned with golden treasures: pale primroses, frilly aconites and starry celandines. Then, in the very moment that Bride and Angus Og declared their intention to marry, the first tree in the forest – a larch – burst into leaf. In its branches, the first bird of spring – a linnet – began to sing, which Bride blessed and named 'the little bird of Bride' (a title it still carries to this day). That day, the first day of February, became known as Imbolc – the festival that marks the beginning of the beginning of spring.

As for the Cailleach, she jumped on her old grey goat and rode away from the growing light and life; back to the distant, dark mountains on the Isle of Skye. There she waits for winter, to regain her seasonal strength. But even though spring is sprung on Bride's Day, the wild world isn't safe from the Cailleach's capricious clutches. Sometimes she rouses herself to reclaim those three days of winter that Angus Og took away, as she foists a fierce, frosty revenge on the land with her blackthorn club.

Spring Cleaning

February takes its name from Februa – a Roman ritual of purification that took place around that month's full moon. As a seasonal festival, it anticipated, and prepared for, the start of spring and the renewal of the growing year. As with orchard wassailing at the end of January, this is a time to cleanse the air of evil influences and wash away the dirt and debris of the old year. The common custom of 'spring cleaning' is both physically and symbolically important at this time of year, particularly using besom brooms made from the thin, flexible twigs of birch trees. In the story of Bride, her transformation from winter captive to spring goddess is precipitated by cleaning the Cailleach's dirty, woollen fleece; stained with the darkness of winter. Eventually, with a helping hand, she accomplishes her task and, in that moment, receives the very first sign of impending spring: a spray of snowdrops.

As White as Snow

The snowdrop, in purest white array,
First rears its head on Candlemas Day.

A widespread European creation myth tells how snow was originally transparent and travelled around the world pleading with each of the flowers to lend their colours. The kindly snowdrop was the only one of them to agree – so it was, snow became white. The two have been firm friends ever since: with snowdrops, also known as snow-piercers, the only flowers allowed to thrive amidst the snow flurries of early February. Although originally alpine flowers, snowdrops are rich in folklore and seasonal associations across Britain and Ireland. Their delicate white petals, almost perfect in their pallid hue, are held as symbols of purity and innocence, as reflected in common names such as white queen, naked maidens and February's fair maids. Their Latin name, *Galanthus nivalis*, means 'milk-flower of the snow'.

Another folk name for snowdrops, Eve's tears, originates from an apocryphal Biblical story, where Eve cried on first feeling the harsh winds of winter after being banished from the Garden of Eden. In pity, God's angels turned Eve's tears into flowering snowdrops as they fell to the ground, to bring her comfort and hope for the brighter days to come. Many public and private gardens around the UK hold annual snowdrop festivals to celebrate their striking seasonal displays in late January and February, with dozens of different flower forms and petal patterns to be seen among the many cultivated varieties.

The Beginning of the Beginning

In the Celtic calendar, the 1st of February is celebrated as Imbolc (pronounced immolk) – the first of the four fire festivals that divide the seasonal year. Traditionally, it marks the inception of spring, with the word itself translating as 'in milk' – reflecting the lactation of ewes at the onset of lambing season at this time. For pastoral societies, highly sensitive to the changing seasons and capricious weather, the return of flowing milk and the replenishment of livestock was – and still is – a significant cause for celebration and marks the restarting of the farming year. Imbolc also heralds the noticeable increase in daylight at this time of year, being exactly halfway between the winter solstice and the spring equinox in the cycle of the seasons.

The shifting balance of the seasons is vividly portrayed in the ancient Celtic myth of the Cailleach and Bride. As the story unfolds, these two archetypal characters ebb and flow in contrast to each other: winter's cruelty giving way to spring's hope. They are sometimes considered as twin aspects of the same goddess – one dark, one light – who together symbolise our struggle to survive and thrive through the changing seasons. In early February, as Bride breaks free from cold captivity and announces her union with the ever-youthful Agnus Og, the natural world begins to stir: the beginning of the beginning of spring. However, old Irish folklore cautions that bright sunny weather at Imbolc means the Cailleach is out gathering firewood, preparing for a longer winter. Better hope for dreary day, instead, and let sleeping hags lie.

The start of the Chinese luni-solar calendar is also timed to mark the waning of winter and the beginning of spring, determined by the first new moon that falls between 21st January and 20th February. Colourful celebrations with food, fireworks and processional dances take place in many communities across the UK each year for Chinese New Year.

From Bride to Brigid

The underlying imperatives for a vibrant celebration at this time of year have endured over time, slowly shifting shape along the way. Imbolc eventually transformed into St Brigid's Day within the church calendar, but the Christian saint still personifies the purity and kindness of early spring – her name itself means 'vigour and virtue'. The cultural bridge between goddess Bride and godly Brigid is wide and well built: both pagan and Christian elements are celebrated together, with a rich range of interwoven folklore and traditions.

St Brigid (also called Brìghde, Brigit or Bridget) is venerated as the 'empty-handed saint', giving away her possessions to those that need them, and credited with many miracles of abundance. One such story tells of her helping the milk maids one morning in the fields, but then blithely giving away the contents of her pail to a poor family on the way home. On returning to the dairy, however, she prayed over the remaining milk and – miraculously – double the usual amount of butter was produced. She is also closely associated with the bounteousness of the natural world and is the patron saint of birthing animals, echoing the seasonal significance of Imbolc.

In Ireland, on 1st February, a whole host of customs around Lá Fhéile Bríde (St Brigid's Day) are still enthusiastically observed. On St Brigid's Eve, lighted candles are placed in windows to welcome her arrival and clothes are left outside to be blessed by her benevolence. On the day itself bread and cakes, especially barmbrack (see this month's recipe), are left on the threshold or by the hearth. An extra setting is laid at the table, to invoke Brigid's generosity and avert hunger in the home for the rest of the year. It's also recognised as a day to make sure that no one goes needy: home-made baked goods are freely shared around the neighbourhood.

Several holy wells in Ireland are dedicated to St Brigid and it has become customary to visit springs and streams at this time of year, as they begin to bubble into life. St Brigid's crosses are traditionally made from rushes gathered from the damp fields and woven into into cross shapes, with either three or four arms. These are hung on doorways of homes and barns to honour the saint and invoke her protection. St Brigid's crosses are also made to be given away to others in the neighbourhood, emulating the saint's inclusivity.

St Brigid's cross hung over the door,
Which did the house from fire secure,
And tho' the dogs and servants slept,
By Brigid's care, the house was kept.

A hagiographical legend reveals the origin of these symbolic rush crosses. While conversing with a pagan chieftain about her faith one day, St Brigid idly picked up rushes strewn on the floor of the hut and slowly wove them into a cross to illustrate the story of Christ's crucifixion. The arms of the crosses, whether three or four, are also said to signify rays of light from the sun, slowly stretching out at this time of year. St Brigid herself is said to have advocated women being allowed to propose marriage. The church authorities only agreed to this happening on the 29th February – once every four years, in a leap year!

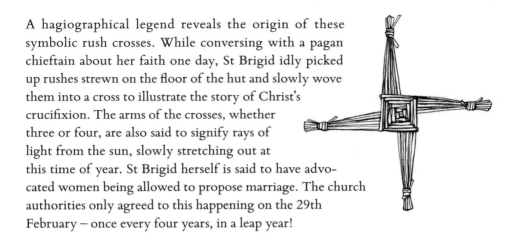

Candlemas: Light Returning

In the Christian calendar, 2nd February is Candlemas Day; also known as the feast of purification, forty days after the birth of Jesus. In medieval times, this was the traditional date when Christmas decorations and Yuletide greenery were brought down and the festive fires of midwinter replaced with candles to celebrate spring's beginning. Before artificial lighting, candles held strong symbolic significance as bringers of light. Candles to be used in the year ahead were blessed during a special church service at Candlemas and were also given as gifts to needy neighbours on this day. Lighted candles were sometimes placed in the ground in gardens and allotments to encourage the light and warmth of spring.

Throughout the wild world, new light is inspiring new life at this time of year. Noticeably, the growing daylight gradually stimulates the awakening of the natural world. Shortly after the snowdrops, there's a rising spring tide of colourful flowers: sweet-smelling violets, pale primroses and golden lesser celandines (also known as 'spring messengers'; 21st February is officially designated as Celandine Day). These first flowers of February, although small and still few in number, feel disproportionately precious. The sweetness of early spring is augmented by a rising symphony of birdsong; reverberating in the still, chilly air. Winter wrens and robins are increasingly joined by a chorus of other neighbourhood residents, finding their voices again: dunnocks and great tits, blackbirds and song thrushes. It's also a good time of year for enjoying the sound of running waters; ringing with energy before plant growth slows the flow. Croaking frogs gather to spawn in garden ponds, while, hidden below ground, badgers give birth in their sunken, earthen setts.

Love is in the Air

This is the day birds choose their mates, and I choose you if I'm not too late!

In Roman times, mid-February was the timing for a lusty celebration called Lupercalia – named after wolves, which were once characterised for their sexual appetite (as evoked in folk tales such as *Little Red Riding Hood*). The Christian church eventually consecrated this time of year through the story of a saint, Valentine, martyred for his faith and sanctified for his faithfulness. On St Valentine's Day, 14th February, women are allegedly able to foretell future husbands by the first feathered creature seen that morning: a goldfinch means a rich spouse; but a sparrow only a poor man; a robin signifies a sailor; whereas a dove augurs a life of happy bliss. According to tradition, birds also fall in love on St Valentine's Day. Certainly many of them can be heard calling for mates at this time, as well as beginning to build their nests.

The Magpie's Nest

One year in February, long ago, Magpie agreed to teach all the other birds how to build a nest. She began by gathering sticks and stems, weaving them together into a round, bowl shape. The crows watched with beady, black eyes and to this day that is how they build their tangled nests.

Then Magpie covered the twigs with thick layers of mud and smoothed the surface. The song thrushes also watched carefully and to this day that is how they build their nests.

Next, she lined the inside of the well-formed nest with soft feathers. The long-tailed tits were huddled together observing and to this day that is how they build their little, feathered nests.

Finally, when no one else was watching, she decorated her nest with pieces of coloured cloth and shiny objects found on the ground. And to this day magpies are always looking for one more bright trinket to finish the decoration of their own, unique nests ...

Cake Month

In the Anglo-Saxon lunar calendar, a full moon in February is named Lenten Moon, which usually commences during this month. In the Christian calendar, Lent represents Jesus's forty days of fasting in the wilderness and is calculated backwards from the date of Easter Sunday. Lent commences on Ash Wednesday with the day immediately before called Shrove Tuesday, from the word 'shrived' – meaning to be absolved from past sins. Traditionally, it is the time to use up food ingredients prohibited during Lent; especially dairy, eggs and fat. Pancakes, in particular, take pride of place on the menu, and even without the widespread observance of Lent any more, Pancake Day remains culturally ingrained in our seasonal calendar. It is perhaps one of the few days of the year where the same food is eaten at the same time, but with lots of variations in how, and with what, they are served. Alongside eating them, some towns and villages still revel in pancake-related fun and games, including competitions and tossing races. In the past it also included an activity known as 'pancake begging' – going from house to house and asking for a tasty gift:

Tippity tippity toe,
Give me a pancake then I'll go!

In both Britain and France, an old version of the gingerbread man folk tale features a tasty pancake rolling away and being chased by several human and animal characters. In French, Shrove Tuesday is called Mardi Gras, which translates as 'Fat Tuesday', and now sparks the start of annual festivals and carnivals around the world. The word carnival itself stems from 'farewell to meat', as animal flesh was also proscribed during Lent. In Scotland, bannock cakes – made from oats, eggs and beef stock – are eaten on this date, known as Bannock Night.

The Anglo-Saxon name for February was Solmonath – sometimes translated as 'mud month', but was thought by Bede to mean the 'month of cakes'. As with St Brigid's Day, offerings of home-made cakes were left by the hearth, in supplication for the success of the new growing season ahead.

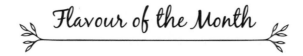

Flavour of the Month

Christmas Decoration
Barmbrack Cake

Thinking about recycling waste one year, we saw the potential for a second innings from the dried apple and orange rounds used as decorations during midwinter merrymaking. Perhaps they would happily rehydrate? Of course they would! So, these inspired the creation of a timely barmbrack recipe to celebrate a Bride's Day meal on 1st February; dusting off winter's grasp, as the light slowly returns. Our recipe spikes and rehydrates the dried winter decorations with whisky and lapsang tea, giving a distinctive smoky tang to this speckled Irish bread-cake, which traditionally hides a ring to decide the next person to get married.

    250g unbleached heritage white flour
    150g currants
    150g mixed dried fruit
    230ml well-brewed black lapsang tea
    110g dark brown muscovado
    70g Laphroaig (or other highly peated whisky)
    25g dried apple slices
    25g dried orange slices
    10g baking powder
    10g mixed spice
    ½ grated nutmeg
    One large free-range egg
    A ring (optional)

- The night before baking, brew a lapsang tea until cool. Add the dried fruits to a bowl and the tea and whisky, and allow them to get to know each other appropriately.
- Preheat the oven to 170°C, lightly butter and line a 900g loaf tin with parchment.
- Combine sifted flour, sugar, mixed spice and the baking powder in a bowl.
- Break the egg into a well in the centre and mix with the dry ingredients. Add a little of the fruit steeping liquid to create a wet batter. Add the remaining fruit, although you may not need all the liquid.
- Drop in the ring, mix once more and pour into the lined baking tin.

- Cook in the centre of the oven for an hour. Test for any uncooked batter and return to the oven if necessary. This cake improves from a couple of days wrapped in beeswax cloth.
- Serve sliced and buttered with tea. If unmarried, watch your teeth.

The Butterfly Bishop

Peter des Roches was the one-time Bishop of Winchester who, despite his status as a church leader, was unequivocally a man of the world – preferring the pursuit of game than tending his flock. One cold and wintry day in February, he went riding through a nearby forest, hunting deer with friends. Late in the day, eager to catch his quarry, he rode on ahead of the rest of the hunting party and soon found himself in an unfamiliar place within the forest. There, to his great surprise, he discovered an imposing stone castle within a clearing among the trees.

A servant invited him inside and there he met the host of the house: none other than King Arthur himself, who welcomed him warmly. After many hours happily feasting and talking with all the assembled knights, King Arthur told the bishop to return to his own world and tell the people of his encounter. Peter asked for a sign, so that he would know he was not dreaming and that others would know he spoke the truth. Arthur told Peter to close and then open his right hand. As he did so, a bright yellow butterfly suddenly flew out of his hand and fluttered animatedly around the hall.

On returning to his own earthly realm, Peter told his people of all that he had seen and heard – that King Arthur lived on, enchanted and ageless, and ready to return when needed most. Seeing their disbelief, he closed and opened his hand to release a bright yellow butterfly, flying freely despite the coldness of the season. News of his miraculous ability – to conjure a butterfly from his hand at any time of year – spread far and wide. Allegedly, anyone who saw one of those butterflies was blessed with grace and good fortune thereafter. Peter himself became rather more goodly and godly after his miraculous meeting with King Arthur, and from then on was known affectionately as the 'Butterfly Bishop'.

Fluttering Weather

Although the shortest of all months, February often seems to encompass two seasons in its weather: one foot firmly rooted in winter, one toe dipping into spring waters. Candlemas Day, at the beginning of the month, has long been used to foretell which of these weather conditions will prevail:

> If Candlemas Day be fair and bright,
> Winter will have another fight;
> If Candlemas day be cloud and rain,
> Winter won't come again.

The incipient stirrings of spring are sometimes stopped in their tracks by heavy frosts or even snowfall in February – allegedly brought by the vengeful Caeilleach, with her blackthorn club. From the end of this month onwards, blackthorn starts to blossom in snow-white profusion and a spell of cold, bitter weather at this time of year is commonly called a 'blackthorn winter'.

On the other hand, there is often a gentle lull in February's weather: mild and moist, giving rise to the copious amounts of mud that our Anglo-Saxon ancestors recognised. In these pockets of warmth, overwintering butterflies awaken from hibernation, such as peacock, small tortoiseshell or red admiral. But the best and the brightest of them all is the buttery yellow Brimstone. The yellow wings of Brimstone butterflies resemble flickering candle flames and to see one at this time of the year is a blessing indeed. According to Tove Jansson, in her Moomin stories, Brimstones are highly auspicious: 'As everyone knows, if the first butterfly you see is yellow the summer will be a happy one.' Symbolically, butterflies represent both the soul and resurrection, and to see one flying in February is a tantalising promise of new life emerging. The visible vital signs are clearly returning, but it's only the very beginning of, perhaps, the most drawn-out season: spring.

Old Roots, New Shoots

BRIDE'S STEAD REVISITED

It's become common practice to ascribe spring to later months in the year, partly due to the cultural influences of North America and mainland Europe, with their continental climates. In maritime Britain and Ireland, however, February has long been recognised as the true beginning of spring, especially in terms of folklore, farming and the natural world. Therefore, the first day of February, with its strong seasonal resonance and tapestry of traditions, feels ripe for being rekindled as a spring celebration – with the open-handed Brigid as a guiding spirit. We could begin by going for a wild walk and gathering long stems of green rushes, willow or hazel – whatever is locally available – for weaving into St Brigid's crosses, hung on the door as replacements for midwinter wreathes. Brigid's Eve is the perfect time to be outdoors as dusk falls, sensing and relishing the seasonal change in twilight's timings. Back home, place lit candles on windowsills, both to symbolise the lengthening light and invite Brigid's blessings into the household. Following the tasty tradition of cake month, make a barmbrack cake, pancakes or bake other teatime treats, to serve up and share with friends or neighbours on the first day in February. Make sure you leave a little offering by the hearth and perhaps a few crumbs for Bride's birds outdoors.

3

March

The man of March he sees the Spring
And wonders what the year will bring
And hopes for better weather ...

Dave Goulder

Hunting the Dawn

In deepest Somerset there was an old woman who lived in an old cottage with a little garden, where she kept a few chickens and a cow. One night, at the end of March, she awoke in the middle of the night, completely convinced that it was already morning and with an overwhelming compulsion to go to market. In the darkness, she dressed and packed her wicker basket with eggs, butter and cream, then set out along the empty country lanes towards the nearby village of Crowcombe.

As she was walking across the gentle contours of a heathland hill she suddenly stopped, as if a spell had been broken, and looked around in bewilderment at the darkness of the night. Then, in the gentle light of the silvery moon rising behind the hill, she saw a small, brown body running swiftly towards her, with long legs and flattened ears. The brown hare zigged and zagged across the hillside with great speed as if being harried and hurried by an unseen hunter. When it reached the spot where the old woman was standing it suddenly stopped, looking up at her with wide, worried eyes. In a flash of conviction, she grabbed hold of the hare and pushed it down into her basket, hastily pulling over some of the straw, before shutting the lid.

Just at that moment the old woman felt a sudden breeze begin to blow from the north, cold, cutting and cruel. Woven within the wind, she could hear the shrill blast of a hunter's horn, followed by the thunder of horses' hooves and the baying of hunting hounds. Silhouetted against the Lenten Moon, the old woman could see a dark huntsman seated upon a jet black horse – a 'Night Mare' – surrounded by a sea of slavering dogs. With a prickling of hairs on the back of her neck, she noticed that the rider's head had long, curved horns. The Wild Hunt swiftly surged towards the old woman, like storm clouds, until the horned rider halted his horse, right in front of her. Steam snorted from the steed's nostrils and the stench of sulphur filled the air. Now she knew for certain who the huntsman was: Old Nick himself. He looked at the old woman with smouldering red embers for eyes and a thin, sneering smile flickered across his lips.

'Old woman, I'm hunting a hare, this night. Long have I hunted her and long has she escaped me. But now she is almost in my grasp. She surely ran past you, so tell me which way she went.'

For a brief moment the old woman felt horribly compelled by the seductive voice to tell the truth of where the hare was hiding. But she quickly quelled her fears and raised her arm, pointing to the west. 'That way ...' she said, as confidently as she could.

'Are you sure?' said the Devil, leaning forward to peer suspiciously into her eyes.

But then, with a lightning crack of his whip, horse and rider were up and away with the dogs flowing around them like living shadows. Only when the sounds of horse and hounds had finally disappeared did the old woman start to relax. Slowly she opened her basket, but inside there were only eggs and cream – the hare had disappeared. Instead, standing suddenly in front of her, was the form of a beautiful young woman, with a shimmering, silvery gown and a golden glow around her head. The old woman didn't know whether she was an angel or a ghost, but when she spoke, she knew it was neither.

'Thank you. Your instincts and your courage have saved me – and the world. For if the Devil and the Wild Hunt had caught me this night, then there would be no dawn on this spring equinox morning and the light would fail to return for the rest of the year.'

The bright being smiled warmly at the old grey woman, then bent down to pick a golden flower from the ground – a starry celandine – and placed it gently in the woman's basket. 'From now on, all will go well with you, all manner of things will go well.'

Then slowly the spirit turned towards the east, and as she did her light began to fade and the outline of her body began to dissolve. But at the exact same moment the golden glow of dawn broke brilliantly over the horizon. The old woman stood for a while, basking in the first rays of sunlight on the spring equinox. Then, she picked up her basket and walked into town to sell her wares, which sold quickly that morning and for a good price, too! And, sure enough, from that day on everything went well for the old woman: the grass grew sweet in her paddock, the cow's milk was creamy and rich, and the hens laid plentiful speckled brown eggs. Everyone that bought her eggs claimed that when cracked open, the yolk inside was as bright and golden as the dawning sun.

Wild

March takes its name from Mars, the full-blooded Roman god of war and agriculture. With winter weather retreating, it was often the month when military campaigns were started or resumed. The month of March also has a long-standing reputation for wild weather, a fierce battleground between the elements. The original Anglo-Saxon name for March was Hraedmonath, in connection to a spring goddess called Hretha, but also translating as the 'month of wildness'. Another Old English name for March was Hlӯda – meaning 'noisy', as in the sounds of storms, characteristic of this time of year. In northern European folk tales, storms are both associated with, and personified by, the Wild Hunt. Although said to sometimes appear on Midsummer's Eve, the Wild Hunt is most likely witnessed in the dark half of the year: between autumnal and vernal equinoxes. Like March weather, the Wild Hunt is capricious and unpredictable and it's best to be indoors when you hear the shrill blast of the Hunter's horn. Although, as the story suggests, it can be dispelled by the light, especially from the dawning sun. Stories of the Wild Hunt sweep into the seasonal significance again in November, as winter storms blow in once more.

One of the old folk names for wood anemones, which appear in swathes beneath forest trees from March onwards, is 'wind flower'. According to ancient Greek mythology, Flora, the goddess of flowers, was jealous of the attention that the nymph Anemone received from her free-flowing husband Zephyr, the god of the west wind. In her fury Flora transformed Anemone into a plant, whose white flowers still tremble when the west wind blows in early spring.

In like a lion, out like lamb.

Stormy weather during March is eventually broken by spells of spring sunshine. In one of Aesop's Fables, the Sun and the Wind compete against each other one day in March, by trying to remove the coat from a traveller's back. The Wind tries his hardest – puffing and blowing in a storm of fury – but only succeeds in making the man pull his coat around himself even more tightly. Then the Sun has her turn and, by shining bright and warm, she eventually wins the contest, as the man removes his own coat. In the past, however, one favourable aspect of March winds was that they helped to dry the wet, muddy fields, allowing farm workers to get back onto the land; giving extra credence to this month's deity, Mars, as the benefactor of agriculture.

The wildness of March has also infused a range of rough and ready recreational games, which traditionally take place around the start of Lent each year. Loosely described as 'feral football', they are gloriously ambiguous about rules, pitches and even goals, with the emphasis firmly on revelry and rivalry. In general, a ball is manoeuvred by two opposing sides from one end of a town to another, usually lasting all day and ending in a local hostelry. Several such games are still played across the UK in February or March, and remain wildly popular.

Borrowing Days

February makes a bridge and March breaks it.

The feisty nature of March is personified in several stories of seasonal conflicts, often resolved through borrowing days from other months. In one tale, March is a wild witch who, on seeing a goatherd take her animals out onto the new growth pastures before the right time, borrows three extra days from February to send icy weather and freeze the poor woman to stone. A similar tale of borrowing days from Ireland features a conceited cow getting its cold, cruel comeuppance ...

The Brindled Cow

Way back then, March was rather shorter than it is now – twenty-eight days, the same as February – and April was three days longer. One day, Old Man March overheard a brindled cow standing in a field boasting to the rest of the herd about how easy it was to withstand the weather of March, compared to the harshness of February. Insulted by such insinuations of weakness, March proceeded to borrow three days from April. During those additional days, March roused himself into a fierce fury: the weather became wild, windy and wet. Soaked to the skin, and flayed by the brutal winds, the poor brindled cow died from exposure to the extreme elements. Since then, March has kept its full complement of thirty-one days, and the weather at the end of the month often proves treacherous to both beast and man…

The Dawning of Spring

The vernal equinox, usually falling on either 20th or 21st March, marks the turning tide of spring, when the light gains ascendency in its seasonal battle with the dark. Day and night are equal lengths on this date and from then onwards the days grow gradually longer, until the peak of the solar cycle at summer solstice. It is commonly ascribed as the start of meteorological spring. Almost as if grabbing the spoils of victory, the clocks also spring forward at the end of March in the UK, giving rise to even longer, lighter evenings as British Summer Time begins.

Lent, a period of roughly six weeks calculated backwards from Easter, has a variable starting date from early February to early March. The etymological origin of the word Lent is 'lengthening', in reference to the noticeable increase in daylight at this time of year. Lent lilies is the folk name for wild daffodils, which flower at this time of year. According to ancient Greek myth they also mark the time when Persephone emerges once more from the underworld to re-join her joyous mother Demeter, the goddess of the harvest (see September).

Other pagan goddesses are also invoked at this time of year: Anglo-Saxon Hretha and Celtic Eostre, who gives both her name and seasonality to the Christian feast of Easter. As illustrated in the Hunting the Dawn story, such deities are associated with dawn, both in terms of daybreak itself and also the dawning of the light half of the year at the spring equinox.

The Leaping Hare

One of the most magical moments in March, if you're lucky, is catching sight of boxing hares. This behaviour has given rise to the hare's reputation for seasonal madness reflected in our language: 'as mad as a March hare' and 'hare-brained'.

It's usually female hares (jills) beating away overzealous males and, although it seems crazed and frenzied, presumably makes perfect sense for the harassed hare in question! Hares are highly reproductive animals and in folklore they have long been seen as potent symbols of fertility and nature's power of renewal in springtime. In ancient mythology hares are the familiars of spring goddesses (mentioned above) as well as the legendary Iron Age warrior queen, Boudica.

You can't run with the hare and hunt with the hound …

Hares are one of the most commonly featured animals in folk tales in Britain and Ireland, where they are often portrayed as tricksters and shape-shifters, in both body and behaviour. In Celtic mythology, the warrior-poet Oisín once injured a hare on its hind leg while out hunting, then carefully followed it back to a patch of brambles. There, among the briars, he discovered a doorway to the Otherworld. Passing through, he saw a bright hall where a beautiful young woman sat in a chair nursing her bleeding leg. The title tales in both March and September chapters of this book reveal hares as shape-shifters and magical, mystical creatures that help hold the balance of light and dark.

One of the best times of year to see a hare is early on a bright March morning, gracefully racing across an open, grassy field or nimbly making its way along a woodland edge. To follow it – with a leap of the imagination – might take you, as with many story characters, into the realm of the fairy folk.

Fairy Gold

Primrose flowers generally reach peak perfection, in both abundance and appearance, during the month of March; one of the brightest treasures of early spring. In former times (and even now in some places) they grew in such rich profusion that they were widely picked for making primrose wine and giving as posies to friends and neighbours. They were so freely available in the wild world that to offer someone less than thirteen flowers was considered a derisory gesture – done only as a deliberate insult.

Primroses are one of the wild plants most strongly associated with the fairy folk, believed to be reawakening at this time of year – in the dawning of spring. Although fairies themselves are rarely seen by human eyes, the ethereal pale yellow of primroses, amidst the still-muted natural world, allegedly indicates the entrances to fairy dwellings. According to folklore, it is possible to catch a glimpse of the Little People by peering carefully over the rim of primrose petals. The fine, yellow pollen from hazel catkins, which flies freely in March as well, is also said to confer an ability to see fairies; whether that be a good thing, or not. In German, the primrose is known as the 'key flower' in reference to its role in opening doorways to other worlds. Planting primroses by the doorstep is thought to invite the blessings of fairy fortune on the household, but they need to be tended carefully in order to avoid such luck turning sour. As the old tales tell, these are golden gifts to be celebrated and shared freely rather than grabbed greedily for ourselves ...

Goblin Combe

One bright morning in March, a small parcel of children spilt out from the Somerset village of Cleeve, down the little lane that leads to Goblin Combe. All winter long it had been too cold and wet to go outside but now the children were filled with pent-up energy and springing enthusiasm to explore the wild woods. The air was still chilly from the night before but slanting sunshine between the trees drew them further into the woods in search of primroses. Here and there between the dark leaf mould of the old year they saw the fresh faces of primrose flowers; shining like fairy gold. Buzzing with excitement, each child began to gather their own posy of primroses, making sure they had at least thirteen or their parents would scold them for bringing back bad luck. However, one little girl, the youngest and smallest of the bunch, was quickly left behind by the rushing tide of children. Being a dreamy sort of girl, and an innocent soul, she soon wandered off the path and into a grove of dark-leaved yew trees.

There she found a deep drift of primroses growing beside a large limestone boulder, their delicate petals newly opening to soak up the spring sunshine. Humming happily to herself, the girl began to pick a posy until, all of a sudden, she became aware that she was alone. Glancing around anxiously, and no longer able to hear the other children, she realised she was completely lost in the deep, dark woods. Tears welled in her eyes and began to drip down on her white cotton dress. Sinking to the ground in distress, she inadvertently laid the little posy of primroses onto the cold, grey rock beside her.

Immediately, there was a loud crack and a flash of golden light. Unwittingly, she had unlocked a secret doorway into the rock that now opened wide as a little line of fairies trooped out, all dressed in clothes of red and green with white owl feathers in their caps. The biggest of the Little People bowed low in front of the startled girl so that his long, grey beard brushed the ground. He stepped forward and presented her with a shining golden sovereign, as large as a ship's wheel in his own diminutive hands. The girl gratefully took the gleaming coin, then followed the fairy king as he led her on a steady march, back through the trees. A few minutes later she was safely back among the other children – who, in truth, had barely noticed her absence – but now stared in wide-eyed wonder at the gold sovereign in her hand. All in a bunch, they ran home to present their primrose posies to their parents and tell of the little girl's encounter with the fairies.

News of fairy gold found in Goblin Combe spread like wildfire through the local area. Eventually it reached the ears of an old conjuror who lived alone in a cold cottage, nursing his greed and selfishness with a constant winter inside his heart. Once he heard the bright rumours of the girl's golden sovereign, he was consumed by the idea of possessing a clutch of such coins for himself. The next day – a wild, windy day towards the end of the month – he went storming through the woods, hastily grabbing a few primroses along the way. He found the old grey rock between the yew trees and casually threw his scrappy posy of petals on the top. A few moments later his greedy grin widened as he saw the secret doorway opening ...

But it wasn't the right time of year anymore, nor had he gathered the right number of primroses – and he certainly wasn't an innocent little soul! So, the Fair Folk didn't give him anything. Instead, they took him away – deep inside the hollow hills of Goblin Combe. And as far as anyone knows, he was never seen in Somerset again.

Several other spring flowers are associated with fairies (see April). In another flowery folk tale from Devon, an elderly woman found favour with the Little People by planting and caring for a bed of tulips in her front garden. Some mornings, in the early spring, she could see their tiny babies cradled in their delicate petals.

Grasping the Nettle

Drink nettle tea in March,
And mugwort tea in May,
And cowslip wine in June,
To send decline away.

Nettles are at their most tender and tasty this month; their new-growth leaves packed with a healthy punch of vitamins and minerals. It's an easy food-plant for foraging: widespread, abundant and often growing near human habitation – although a little care is needed when grasping the nettle! Nettle's Latin name *Urtica* comes from the verb 'to burn' and folk names include Devil's leaf and weed of Mars – the prickly god who lends his name to March. The cure for nettle stings, and perhaps one of the few commonly used herbal remedies nowadays, is rubbing a dock leaf on the affected skin. Allegedly, loudly reciting the following phrase helps: Nettle in, dock out; dock rubs nettle out!

There is an annual nettle eating competition in Dorset, held for many years at the Bottle Inn, but recently moved to Dorset Nectar orchard. Allegedly it originated from an argument between two farmers over the size of their nettle patches. If eating *raw* nettles isn't to your taste, there are lots of ways to cook up a nettle feast, including the seasonal recipe below. Other simple culinary ideas include nettle soup, nettle bread and nettle tea.

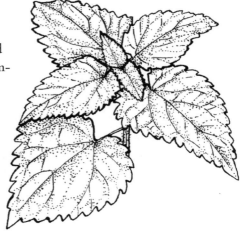

Green Shoots Dressing

Seeing the first green shoots of March is a gleeful time for all wild food enthusiasts. Perhaps, the brightest green of them all is the three-cornered leek, easily dismissed as (poisonous) daffodils. Cut across the width and you'll see the stem has three corners, emitting a delicate and onion-like scent. It can be found among rocky walls and garden edges, often close to the first shoots of the instantly recognisable stinging nettle and pungent mint. The bitter-tasting, toothed leaves of dandelions drive upwards in verges, meadows and lawns. All of these foraged plants have abundant flavour, nutrients and minerals, and can be easily found on a springtime walk. It's well worth gathering a little of each to make a bright and tasty salad dressing. Don't forget your washing up gloves; they are excellent protection from the stinging nettle.

To capture the spring colour and flavour, we must turn to a valuable kitchen technique: blanching. Plunging herbs or anything chlorophyll-rich into rapidly boiling water, followed by ice water, will retain the plant's vibrancy. In this case, we also denude the stinging hairs of the nettle, freeing up a pain-free path to its beta carotene, vitamin C, vitamin E and silica nutrients.

An open handful of each: three-cornered leek, nettle and mint leaves
Half an open handful of dandelion leaves
A good dash of sherry vinegar
Good-quality olive oil
Sea salt
Black pepper

- Wash all leaves well, and de-stem the nettle and mint.
- Roughly slice the long three-cornered leek to a similar size as the nettle leaves.
- Have a large bowl of water with plenty of ice ready. Employing a large pan filled with water at a rolling boil, add a teaspoon of salt, then all the leaves and cook for ninety seconds.
- With a slotted spoon, transfer the leaves to the ice bath for their trip to ice town.

- Once chilled, remove the leaves and dry well between two tea towels.
- Add the leaves with oil and vinegar to a blender, spin until combined, and season with salt and pepper.
- To savour the irresistible scents, use the dressing immediately to accompany oriental leaf salads, freshly made soups and, of course, roast lamb. Store leftovers in the fridge for the next day.

Heavenly Gardens

March has a good crop of saints days with horticultural connections to help celebrate being out and about again in the garden this month. The saints start marching in on 1st March with St David's Day (Dewi Sant), the patron saint of Wales, having two garden delights — daffodils and leeks — to honour his feast day. Bright yellow daffodils begin to grace the garden in March — matching the colour of new-born chicks and traditionally should only be brought indoors once the first hens' eggs have hatched. Leeks reach both the end of their harvest period and the start of their sowing dates this month. One proud Welsh legend asserts that on the eve of a battle St David advised his followers to wear leeks on their caps to distinguish themselves from the Saxon enemies. Suitably seasonal and proudly patriotic, Glamorgan sausages are made from leeks and Caerphilly cheese.

Next, St Patrick's Day is celebrated on 17th March, when it's traditional to wear a green shamrock in honour of the affectionately held patron saint of Ireland. The term shamrock is not botanically precise — arising from the Irish word seamróg, which translates as 'young clover'. According to legend, Patrick used the tri-foliate structure of clover to explain the Holy Trinity to his followers. At this time of year, the new growth of clover, and other herb-like plants, is vivid, vibrant green; the colour of the Emerald Isle itself. Green is widely worn in Ireland on St Patrick's day to celebrate the season and (allegedly) appease the leprechauns. Traditionally, this is also the date for planting out seed potatoes. Other customary gardening dates this month governed by saints' days include: 12th March (St Gregory's Day) for setting onions and 21st March (St Benedict's Day) for sowing peas.

Ladies of Virtue

The 25th March is Lady Day in the church calendar and marks the day that the birth of Jesus was foretold to Mary by archangel Gabriel, nine months before Christmas. Lady Day was once the official start date of the new year in the UK, which is still reflected in the beginning of the financial year on 6th April – Old Lady Day, after the change to the calendar (see Introduction). Another virtuous lady, Lady Mabella, is remembered on this day as the originator of the Tichborne Dole: an ongoing annual custom (once one of many) to distribute food to the parish poor at a time of year, commonly known as the 'hungry gap'.

The Tichborne Dole

Over 800 years ago, in the village of Tichborne in Hampshire, there lived a wealthy woman named Lady Mabella, who was kind and compassionate to all. Sadly, she suffered from a debilitating and progressive illness and so, fearing the imminent end of her life, asked her husband – Sir Roger Tichborne – if he would care for the poor of the parish after she was gone. Unfortunately, Sir Roger was far less charitable than his wife and agreed only to provide the food that could be grown on an area of land that she could walk whilst carrying a burning branch from the fire. Undaunted by the perversity of the task, Lady Mabella summoned her strength and set out with her maidservants on a typically blustery day in March. As she began her walk, however, the wild winds miraculously died down and the torch she was carrying burned brightly and steadily. In the end Mabella bravely managed to crawl around an area of 23 acres; much to the chagrin of her husband, who assumed the flames would burn far more quickly. The piece of land was duly assigned to grow wheat to produce flour to be given away to the needy every year on Lady Day, 25th March. Sensing Sir Roger's reluctance to keep his promise, however, Lady Mabella also uttered a curse on her death bed that the house would fall down if the dole was ever discontinued. To this day, the house still stands…

Old Roots, New Shoots

SIGNS OF THE TIMES

After the delicate promises of primroses, a spring-tide of yellow laps at the edges of the wild world: dandelions shine like gold coins along the verges and the gorse bushes are festooned with coconut-scented flowers – kissing season is puckering up. Above the open fields, skylarks flutter up to the roof of the world and pour out a mellifluous melody as sweet as spring sunshine itself. The surging singing of resident birds is combined with the first seasonal migrants winging their way here, to their summer homes. Perhaps the most well-known and anticipated of early springtime heralds is the sound of the chiffchaff, with its distinctive two-tone tune proclaiming: *spring is sprung!* This simple rallying call is followed by more elaborate choruses of willow warblers and blackcaps in late March onwards. Freshly painted butterfly wings begin to drift through greening gardens – Holly Blues and Orange Tips – to join the larger species that overwintered as adults and appeared earlier in the year. Adders, emerging from hibernation in March, can sometimes be seen in sunny spots on heathland and woodland edges in Britain (but not Ireland, where St Patrick legendarily banished them). Almost snake-like themselves, the fiddle-heads of ferns also slowly unfurl in the incipient sunshine.

March is a magical month for undertaking your own, localised 'spring watch': seeking out and celebrating the reappearing wonders of the natural world. The slow procession of signs of spring allows for an annual check-up on personal lists of favourite firsts: blossom, birds, butterflies and many more. It's a great opportunity to visit our best-loved locations, wander the wild edges of our neighbourhood and revel in the soundings and

sightings of spring. It's worth making a note of when each species is heard or seen to compare seasonal changes over the years.
If you're lucky, you might even catch sight of a springing hare,
carrying the dawn in its light, lithe body.

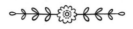

4

April

Twas on one April morning, just as the sun was rising,
Twas on one April morning, I heard the small birds sing.

The Green Mist

Amongst the wet meadowlands and fertile farmland of East Anglia, there's always been a strong belief in the influence of the Fair Folk. In spring, it's said, the fairies stir from their hidden hollows to cast their spells of revival – awakening the earth and arousing the wild world. Their seelie seasonal magic is hidden from view within a verdant veil, known as the 'Green Mist'.

In one fenland village, not *that* long ago, there lived a farmworker's daughter who had grown into a bright and sprightly young woman. Until recently, she'd been the very essence of life and light, much-loved by her proud parents and much-admired by the young men of the parish. That winter, however, she was stricken with a lingering malaise that continued for months without remedy or respite. Her parents fretted dreadfully to see their daughter – once in such rude, ramping health – become so listless and lifeless. Doctors and wise women were all at a loss to either explain or alleviate her debilitating illness and, as the winter months wore on, she worsened. In the end she was so frail and fragile in health that she could barely walk around the house.

Eventually, the long, cold winter softened into spring, as it always does. One day in early April, standing by the open doorway, she smiled, weakly, to see the very first cowslips flowering in the garden – their buttery yellow petals held aloft on delicate stalks. Beyond the garden, across the river valley, she could see the swirling haze of the Green Mist gently lapping around the crops in the fields edges and the flowers of the meadow. Her heartbeat quickened as a hopeful thought floated into her mind: perhaps the Green Mist will bring me back to health again, after this long winter of decay. 'Even if I only lived as long as these cowslips by my window, I'd be happy with such a lease of life,' she whispered into the soft spring air.

On hearing those words, her mother tutted loudly and ushered the daughter quickly back inside the house. 'Hush my dear! The Others have sharp ears and always drive a hard bargain for their fickle magic ...' But the wish-words were already spoken. In response, *perhaps*, there was a ripple in the Green Mist as it surged a little higher.

The next day brought a perfect spring morning: bright and warm, with slanting sunlight flooding through the windows of the cottage. Feeling distinctly stronger, the daughter sat outside by the front door in a wicker chair, savouring the warm, spring sunshine on her pale face. The following day was equally fine and by then she was able to complete a circuit of the front garden under her own steam. By the end of the week, she was almost back to her old self again – to the relief and delight of her parents; although she had a wistful dreaminess to her demeanour they hadn't noticed before. And if the weather turned cloudy or cold, she would suddenly rush back inside the house, as if she'd seen a ghost.

As the cowslips in their front garden flourished, so her radiant health and lively spirit shone, drawing appreciation from passing neighbours. One day a young man from the village – an aspiring admirer – came by to introduce himself. Standing there at the front door, with nesting house martins whirling around his head, he suddenly remembered he'd neglected to bring a gift. He caught sight of the colourful cowslips and, without thinking, bent down to pick a little posy of the golden flowers. When the daughter opened the door, her eyes quickly fell upon the cowslips in his outstretched hand and she let out an instinctive, audible gasp. The door was hastily slammed shut as she ran inside, leaving the young man wide eyed and wondering.

That same day she heard a cuckoo calling in the river valley, a sound resonating with both sweetness and sadness, for the birds leave so soon after arriving. Although her physical health remained intact over the next few weeks, the young woman became increasingly obsessed with the state of the cowslips in the garden. She fussed constantly over their watering and weeding. But in her heart she knew that the turning of the seasons cannot be delayed for long. Sure enough, as spring strengthened into summer, the yellow flowers of the cowslips faded and the green leaves lost their vigour. By Midsummer's Day they were all gone – and so was she.

Cowslip Time

The common name 'cowslip' refers to what slides out of the back end of grazing cattle, rather than clumsy cows, as the plant grows well in manured meadows. Other folk names for cowslips allude to its connections with the Fair Folk, including: fairy bells, fairy cups and fairy basins. The delicate rosy spots at the base of the flowers were once known as 'fairy favours'; echoing the Green Mist story.   They are also known as St Peter's Keys, referring to a legend that Heaven's gatekeeper once dropped his golden keys, which fell to the earth and sprang up as cowslips. Cowslip wine, traditionally made at this time of year, is a drinkable delicacy and in past times the flowers were gathered into bloomy balls called 'tissty-tossties' – to be tossed in the air while spelling out the name of prospective lovers.

In recent times, cowslips have declined steeply on farmland and are best seen in gardens and roadside banks, where they can still be profuse in places. They were once a common component of water meadows, where a flush of nutrient-rich river water facilitated lush spring growth for early grazing, and a rich habitat for wildflowers. It's striking to find a British folk tale so directly and distinctly linked to one particular plant. The lifecycle of the cowslip adds another layer of seasonal specificity to the story: its golden flower stalks first flourish at the beginning of April and continue on into late June, before fading away. Cowslips have associations with 'heart-sickness' and death of the young, perhaps because they appear to hang their heads sadly. Like spring, and perhaps life itself, cowslips are beautiful but fleeting. The flowers stalks are sometimes referred to as bells, which chime the hours of life. Our seasons are sweet but short-lived, passing quickly, especially if we try to hold on to them too tightly.

Spring Greens

After the flash of gold from flowers in early spring, green is increasingly the dominant natural colour during April. Green shoots transform the brown earth as a surging spring tide floods fields and farms. Woodlands and river valleys are also cloaked with leafy hues as the 'Green Mist' seeps outwards, widening the miracle of growth. Folk tales about the Fair Folk advise caution at this time of year in our dealings with the Others, as their supernatural powers can be both benign and baleful. Like the fairies themselves, British weather can be cruel and capricious – April can make fools of us all.

'Til April is dead, change not a thread.

Another famous folk tale from East Anglia recounts the sudden appearance of two strange children, a boy and a girl, with completely green skin and hair, who could only eat green food. While the girl survived in our world, and eventually lost her green colour, the boy quickly withered and died, just like the young woman in the Green Mist story. Hope rises in spring, but young shoots are at their most tender and new life is precarious. Many of our treasured spring heralds, from cowslips to cuckoos, are as sensitive and vulnerable as the season itself: not only to the vagaries of weather but to longer-term changes in habitats and climates. Springtime can make us aware of losing the things we most love.

Stripping the Willow

All round my hat I'll wear the green willow,
All around my hat for a twelve month and a day.

Willows are among the first trees to 'green up' in April and in folklore (and folk songs) they represent loss and sadness – *weeping* willows. The phrase 'wear the green willow' originates from those recently bereaved, or with lovers away at sea or war, wearing a stem of willow in their hat or on their clothes. Willows can also be used for wish-making: tie a gentle knot in the thin supple branches of a new growth willow and make a supplication to the Fair Folk. Be aware, however, it is beholden upon the wish-maker to come back and untie the knot if the wish is fulfilled, to avoid offending the fairies! Allegedly, 'knock on wood' stems from the custom of whispering wishes into willow trees and asking for favour. The phrase 'the wind in the willows' made famous by Kenneth Graham's eponymous novel, also refers to the movement, and magic, of the fairy folk among the green trees.

There are many myths and legends about why weeping willows have their characteristic sad, drooping shape. These include hanging weapons in their branches at the cessation of warfare and their sorrow at witnessing Adam and Eve's expulsion from the Garden of Eden. In Britain and Ireland, willow wands have long been used as substitute materials for weaving into crosses on Palm Sunday; a celebration of welcoming in good news.

Opening Time

February finds spring, March draws it out and April luxuriates in it.

April's name comes from the Latin word *apriere*, meaning 'to open'. In the wild world now, flowers open their petals to pollinators, trees open their leaves to the sun and birds open their mouths to sing, then feed their open-mouthed chicks. It's also a time when we welcome old friends with open arms: the next wave of summer migrants – swallow and swift, cuckoo and nightingale – arrive at our shores on open wings and seem to bring the warmth of southern countries with them. One swallow doesn't make a summer, the old saying goes, but certainly the first one brings great cheer – a feeling that all's well in the world again. Traditionally, 15th April is earmarked as Swallow Day, although the average arrival time to our (southern) shores is now around two weeks earlier. Our fond feelings for the return of these summer heralds are so culturally ingrained, they have woven their way into seasonal stories and creation myths ...

The Swallow's Tail

When God created the Garden of Eden, Lucifer also arrived on earth; as a fallen angel. Knowing that the Devil would spoil paradise, God banished him from Eden, with two bright angels placed at the garden gates to guard it by day and night. However, the Cunning One saw that all of God's creatures were able to pass through the gates freely, so he approached each of them and asked for assistance. But none of them would dare break God's commands and help

the Devil. All except one: Snake!
Snake was seduced by Satan's
sweet promise: 'If you help
me, I'll make sure that you
get to eat the sweetest meat
in the whole of creation –
the flesh of Adam and Eve.'

Snake agreed and the
deal was sealed. The Devil
shrank down to the size of a
seed and stepped inside Snake's
mouth, hiding behind one of
its fangs. And that's how the Devil
entered the Garden of Eden, unseen by
God's guardian angels. He made his way to
Eve, sitting by herself under the shade of a tree, and from inside the serpent's
mouth the Devil spoke to Eve: tricky, sticky words of temptation. Well, the rest
of that story is well known; sin entered into paradise. But that's not the end of the
tale for Snake: he hadn't yet received his promised reward ...

The next day Snake was slithering through the long grass to where Adam
and Eve lay sleeping, naked, in the Garden of Eden. He was about to take a delicious bite of their sweet flesh, when a bird with dark blue wings fluttered down
and landed in front of him. When Swallow heard Snake's story, she laughed.
'Ha! Everyone knows the Devil is a liar. Let's put the matter to the test: we'll
ask Mosquito to taste the flesh of all God's creatures, great and small, and report
back on which one is the sweetest ...'

So little Mosquito, without any need for persuasion, set out to taste every
animal in creation. As she returned to the Garden of Eden, Swallow, suspecting
that the answer would indeed be Mankind, swiftly intercepted Mosquito before
she could tell the others. In a flurry she darted forward and pecked out Mosquito's
tongue; from that moment on, all Mosquito could say was: zzzzzzmmm!

Swallow told Snake that Mosquito had said the sweetest flesh belonged to ...
Frog! Snake knew he'd been tricked and with surprising speed lunged forward,
mouth open, towards Swallow. In a flash, she flew up in the air just as Snake's
fangs grabbed the end of her long tail. And that's why, to this day, swallows
have forked tails! And that's also why there's still a great friendship between
Mankind and Swallow-kind. Each year we eagerly look out for their forked
tails trailing through the sky in early April. And in return we happily let them
nest in the eaves of our homes.

The Nightingale's Tongue

Don't you hear the fond tale
Of the sweet nightingale,
As she sings in those valleys below?

The nightingale, perhaps possessing the sweetest of all spring songs, is also honoured with its own origin story. In the beginning, when the Creator painted all the birds' feathers with their final flourishes of colour, the little brown nightingale was the last in the queue. By then all the paints were used up, except one dab of gold left on the brush – just enough to cover the nightingale's tongue. Since then, as soon as nightingales return in April, they proudly show off their golden tongues, in a virtuoso performance of colourful song from dusk to dawn.

Gone Cuckoo!

In April, come he will.
In May, he's here to stay.
In June, he changes his tune.
In July, he prepares to fly.
In August, away he must.

If we're lucky, the distinctive calls of cuckoos are first heard in April, traditionally on St Tiberius Day (15th April). Despite declining numbers, they remain one of our most widely celebrated birds, in poetry, song and story. In Celtic mythology, cuckoos were chosen as messengers between our world and *Tir-nan-Og*, the land of Eternal Youth. In their given roles as intermediaries for the gods they don't have time to rear their own chicks on Earth, so instead they lay them in the nests of other birds, before flying away again on divine duties. Hearing the first cuckoo of the year is still a much-anticipated seasonal marker and there's an abundance of superstitions associated with hearing the first cuckoo: whatever you're doing when you hear the first call, you'll do for the rest of the year. To be standing on soft ground at the time is lucky, but firm ground means hard times; turning over the money in your pockets will ensure there'll always be plenty; counting the number of calls will tell the number of years until your wedding day.

There are several folk tales that provide foundation stories for annual events celebrating the April arrival of the cuckoo. Towednack in Cornwall still holds an annual feast in late April, that stems from the tale of a villager once putting a hollow log on the fire, whereby a cuckoo suddenly flew out, bringing warmer weather. A similar Sussex legend relates how a local character called Dame Heffle released cuckoos from her basket every April, which now underpins an annual Cuckoo Fair in Heathfield. The Marsden Cuckoo Festival in Yorkshire, is based on the story of foolish locals trying to stop cuckoos from leaving the area. This humorous folk tale has many geographical variants across England, including Wareham in Dorset; retold below.

On April Fool's Day (1st April) it was once common custom to call someone a 'cuckoo' if you caught them out with a trick. The word was widely used to designate a foolish person, as in 'gone Cuckoo', allegedly because of the birds simplistic, oft-repeated call. The similarly used word in Scots is 'gowk'. Two once-common plants, cuckoo pint and cuckoo flower, are named after their synchronous flowering with calling cuckoos; although increasingly, in many places, plants are now unserenaded. Cuckoo flower is also known as lady's smock, an allusion to young lovers kissing among spring flowers in late spring (see May). Cuckoo spit is a folk name for the frothy secretion exuded by immature planthoppers, which, coincidentally, is often found on the stems of lady's smock.

The Wareham Cuckoo

Every spring, a cuckoo arrived in the Dorset town of Wareham to call from the high branches of a willow tree. The townsfolk loved hearing the bird's two-tone tune as the herald of warmer weather and happier times. By late summer, the cuckoo would always fly away again with the passing of the seasons. Most people accepted the natural way of the world, enjoying the sweet sound of the cuckoo while it lasted. However, there were three headstrong old men who thought they could change things: they planned to trap the cuckoo so that spring would last forever in Wareham! That year, at the beginning of April, they painstakingly built a tall tower from Purbeck stone all around the tree where the cuckoo sat and sang. But the foolish men didn't think to put a roof on the tower and by the beginning of July the cuckoo simply opened its wings to fly up and out and away.

Easter Eggs

Easter is the ultimate 'variable feast', with an antiquated and complicated date calculation based on the intersection of solar and lunar calendars. It is determined as the first Sunday after the full moon on or after the spring equinox and as such ranges between 22nd March at the earliest and 25th April at the latest. According to Anglo-Saxon monk Bede, the Christian festival Easter takes its name from the pagan goddess of Eostre (sometimes called Ostara), a deity associated with spring and dawn (see March). In Celtic mythology, Eostre once rescued a hare trapped in snow by turning it into a bird. Once in its new form, the hare continued to lay eggs like a bird – which is why the Easter bunny delivers eggs! Folklore dictates you shouldn't work on Good Friday (if you can help it) but it is an auspicious day for baking, especially hot cross buns, and collecting eggs.

Birds, both residents and returning migrants, lay their eggs during April, which are beginning to open by the end of the month. The Anglo-Saxon name for a full moon in April is Egg Moon, reflecting this egg-laying season. Saxon graves also sometimes contained eggs, thought to represent the hope of being reborn in the afterlife, and the egg is widely regarded as a symbol of rebirth, recycling and the wholeness of life. Because of the prohibition from consuming eggs and other rich foods in Lent, they were often the first tasty treats to be eaten at Eastertide. Their luxuriousness has been enhanced over time to today's chocolate Easter eggs.

The seasonal importance of both eggs and Easter has fostered a wide range of egg-related annual customs over time, some still widely enjoyed. Decorating hard-boiled (or blown) eggs is a wonderfully accessible creative craft, often reflecting the pastel colours and speckled patterns of birds' eggs in the wild world. Decorated eggs can then be used for rolling down grassy hills on common land and public parks on Easter morning. Egg tapping, also known as egg jarping, is a traditional Easter game played by two competitors knocking the pointed end of hard-boiled eggs together to see which one cracks first (the loser), with the world championships held in Peterlee in County Durham every year. A similar game called egg shackling is played by shaking eggs with names written on them in a sieve, until one is left uncracked and declared the winner. Pace Egging refers to a type of mummers' play (see December) still performed in several places at Easter time, particularly in north-west England. Pace derives from the Latin word *pasch*, referring to the passion of Christ at Eastertide.

Here's one, two, three jolly lads all in one mind,
We are come a-Pace-Egging and I hope you'll prove kind.

St George and the Dragon

Once, in England's green and pleasant land, there was a village situated beneath a round hill. But, the place and its people were overshadowed by the tyranny of a dreadful dragon. Each year, in spring, the green-scaled serpent would rouse from its subterranean slumbers and descend upon the village. In the beginning the villagers abated its greed with livestock, cattle and sheep, but eventually the dragon demanded more than meat. Every year the villagers drew lots to choose a sacrificial young bride who, wearing a white wedding dress and blue sash, was taken to the entrance of the dragon's cave. The villagers bitterly lamented the loss of their daughters, but were in thrall to the dragon's ferocity. Then one year, just before the spring sacrifice, a soldier from the Roman army arrived in the village, introducing himself as George. On hearing the tale of the village's plight, George offered to take the young woman's place and so, wearing the chosen maiden's blue sash, he rode out to confront the dragon at its lair.

Not far from the village, George came to a small spring, bubbling up from the roots of a willow tree, where he stopped to fill his bottle and offer up a prayer for faith and courage. When he arrived at the entrance of the cave, he was immediately greeted by a blast of flame and smoke as the dragon emerged to face his foe. Rather than draw his sword, however, George uncorked his flask and flung the spring water over the beast's body. The fierce firedrake was immediately calmed by the holy water, and a few hours later George returned to the village leading the dragon by the blue sash around its neck. There was great rejoicing among the village for the miracle of the dragon's defeat. George himself was heralded as a saint – the protector and patron of England!

As for the dragon itself, some say it settled down on the fertile grassland beside the village and fell asleep. Over many years it melded into the lay of the land, its serpentine body becoming a river that roared down from the hill in spring. Each year, in late April, the villagers made a little straw doll with a tiny bluebell sash, which was offered to the rising river as a token sacrifice to the green dragon and in remembrance of St George.

By George!

In the church calendar, 23rd April is celebrated as the feast day of St George. Originally from Cappadocia, in modern Turkey, he's become a well-loved and widely recognised figure – not only as the patron saint of England, but also several other places, including Ethiopia, Catalonia and Georgia (of course!). Once widely celebrated in the Middle Ages, St George's Day festivities have unfortunately faded with time. However, in some parts of England, morris dancing still marks the occasion outside pubs as well as a revival of seasonally specific mummers' plays, telling varying versions of the time-honoured tale of St George and the dragon.

Bluebells, which come into flower from the end of April onwards, were traditionally worn on St George's Day to mark the occasion. The UK holds up to half of the world's population of bluebells, so they can rightly be thought of as national treasures themselves. The patron saint of England also has a species of edible fungus named after him, St George's mushroom, which appears around the date of his feast day and provides a tasty treat.

Flavour of the Month

Coddled Eggs with
St George's Mushroom and Wild Garlic

There's a stunning natural reward in the fields and orchards if you take the time to look in warmer weather in March and April: St George's mushrooms. Its underground mycelium nourishes the grass, which grow in rings visibly taller than the surrounding pasture; sometimes 15ft wide. Carefully root around in these humid, grassy microclimates and you'll likely find the pearly white and light cream, tightly gilled fruiting bodies of the mushroom. As you get close, the mealy and cucumber-scented tones are often vivid – one of the reasons that it is so highly prized as a foraged food. Before even considering eating any mushroom you gather, carefully photograph them in as much detail as possible, caps, undersides, gills and stems. Double-check with a reputable guidebook or local expert to confirm all the characteristics. It's worth reaching out to mushroom-identifying groups online for confirmation, too. As Terry Pratchett wisely noted: 'All mushrooms are edible, some only once.'

At the same time of year in the woods, where bluebells cast their mesmerising blue shimmer, wild garlic is abundant. Its scent, garlicky and chive-like, can be used to safely identify it. Gathering a few of its aromatic leaves will do no harm to the plant, but be mindful not to uproot its bulb and there'll be a patch to revisit in years to come.

You'll need an egg and a ramekin per person and a sided oven tray filled with boiling water, to sit the ramekins in for their gentle coddling in the oven. Set your oven close to 150°C.

Slice and fry together St George's mushroom and wild garlic in butter, until lightly wilted but still moist. Season with a dash of sea salt. Cover the base of each buttered ramekin with this spring-scented foraged finery.

Crack an egg (hen or duck) into each ramekin, trying to keep the yolk intact, then grate black pepper on top. Carefully slide the tray into the oven and check the eggs after six minutes, aiming for a soft yolk and lightly white surface.

Serve with buttered bread and a dash of cider vinegar – a cut above perfect. Miniature egg moons, of which even St George would be proud.

Here Be Dragons

In seasonal mythology, dragons symbolise the dark forces of winter, which are overcome each year by the power and hope of spring; just as legendary St George defeated his scaly foe with holy faith. Dragons also epitomise the surging power of nature at this time of year, as a green pulse pushes out from beneath the earth and fern fronds unfurl like little serpents. Rivers, roaring with meltwater, take on serpentine power and in medieval England spring-flooding rivers were often referred to as 'dragons'.

In a local legend, called the Lambton Worm, a formidable giant serpent capable of regeneration, is eventually cut into small pieces that fall into the river. There, in the rush and tumble of the water, the still-living pieces of dragon are held, unable to reassemble and reform. The story suggests, perhaps, learning to live with, rather than dominate, the elemental powers of nature.

In most versions of the hagiographical legend, St George slays the dragon, as portrayed in many pieces of art, but, in this account, he succeeds by taming the beast with a blue sash. Symbolically, blue is the colour of purity and innocence – it's the colour of the Virgin Mary's robe, as well as being the only colour (other than white) worn by brides. The Knights of the Garter, dedicated to St George and upholding chivalry, wear a blue ribbon as their emblem. In the wild world, it's also the colour of wide-open skies and deep blue waters, with their cool, calming influences.

Old Roots, New Shoots

GREEN GEORGE

Romany gypsies, perhaps travelling from east to west in St George's footsteps, brought with them their own seasonal celebration in late April, when spring growth is at its most riotous and rampant. The centrepiece of the spring celebration was a willow tree hung with decorations and presents. Pregnant women would place an item of clothing beneath the tree – if a green leaf fell on it, they would be blessed with an 'easy' childbirth; perhaps reflecting that willow is a natural source of pain-killing aspirin. Boys would dress up in costumes of living leaves to represent Green George, the spirit of spring, echoing the Green Man.

A revival of such celebrations on St George's Day offers an opportunity to weave together some of the varied strands of nature and culture, dragon and saint, as well as reclaim a distinctiveness in seasonal and national identity at a peak time of year. The name George originates from the Greek *Georgos*, meaning 'earth-worker', or farmer, which seems fitting for an earthy seasonal celebration. It might be as simple as a group walk or shared picnic in a local bluebell woodland, amongst lime-green tree leaves and unfolding ferns. It could involve decorating a willow tree with coloured ribbons and/ or gently tying knots in its branches to make wishes and remember loved ones. Music, mummers' plays and morris dancing always bring a communal occasion to life, building up an appetite for a feast of foraged food: wild garlic, tender beech leaves and St George's mush-rooms (making sure you know what to look for!). Dandelion flowers are also traditionally picked on St George's Day, when they are at their most fragrant, to be fermented into a light, flowery wine ready for drinking on Midsummer's Day.

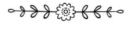

Time Flies

The 25th April is the feast day of St Mark, who is distinguished by having his own insect named after him – St Mark's Fly – which first appears around this time. It's a distinctive, black, dangly legged creature, also known among anglers as the hawthorn fly; referring to the May blossom about to burst in the hedgerows.

5

May

As I roamed out one May morning, one May morning so early,
'Twas down by the side of a shady green tree;
O there I beheld a most beautiful damsel,
She sat there a-sighing all underneath a tree.

Thomas the Rhymer

Thomas was the young laird of a large estate of forests, fields and farms in the Scottish Borders. Being also handsome and single, there were many eligible and elegant young women who came visiting, hoping to win his affection. But none succeeded, for Thomas was in love with the land: the wind-swept hills, the rolling rivers and the leafy green forests. Most of the work in tending the woodlands and farmland was undertaken by local villagers, whom Thomas treated well, with decent housing and wages. And four times a year, at the start of each of the seasons, he arranged a lavish feast for all the workers' families to make merry. The biggest, and best, of these seasonal festivities was Beltane, at the eve of summer, when the warmth of the sun was returning and the wild world was frothing with flowers.

Early on May Morning, garlands of green vegetation were hung from the doorways of every house. Young women went to the meadows to wash their faces in the dew and young men gathered posies of fresh flowers – marigolds and cowslips, bluebells and lady's smock – to give to their sweethearts. After milking the cows, the rest of the day was given over to a banquet of roast lamb and spring vegetables, washed down with freshly brewed ale; all served on the lawn in front of the manor house. Afterwards, a great bonfire was lit and the revellers, wearing crowns of green leaves with white blossom, danced around the flames. At the end of the night, some would throw their wreaths across the grass and hope that the fairy folk would use them for their own dancing, and bring a blessing for the year ahead. But on May Day that year, Thomas was disconnected and distant. He left soon after the feasting and before the dancing; to the disappointment of several ambitious admirers.

He went roaming across the fields, his feet unerringly finding their way to the edge of the fresh-leafed forest. There he walked slowly, enjoying the arboreal atmosphere, until he found himself among a sea of luminous bluebells. Their sight and scent were so overwhelming that Thomas began to feel dizzy and disorientated. He sank down besides an old hawthorn tree, with its creamy white flowers glowing in the gloaming and their heady perfume hanging in the air. Soon his eyelids began to droop as he drifted away ...

As he slept beneath the May tree, a single delicate petal fell slowly through the air and landed gently on his lips. He awoke suddenly to the sound of tinkling bells, as if the bluebells themselves were ringing. But looking up he saw a milk-white mare, with jingling silver bells attached to the reins, and the most beautiful woman he'd ever seen sitting in the saddle. She was wearing a diaphanous dress the colour of fresh beech leaves, with a riding cape of darker green around her shoulders and a silver horn hanging from her side. Her hair was as black as a raven's wings, her lips glistened as red as haws and her eyes – firmly fixed on his – matched the emerald hue of the woods. Thomas's heart missed a beat, then with a sudden surge he sprang to his feet. 'Are you the Queen of Heaven?'

She laughed lightly, her voice lilting like a nightingale: 'No, I am not that particular Lady. But I am indeed Queen of my own realm and on this day of May magic I am able grant you a wish ...'

'I wish for a kiss!' He said boldly, without hesitation.

The green lady smiled, then leaned down from her saddle and stretched towards him until their lips touched. But in that tender moment the spell was broken: her lips became dry and wrinkled and the rider faded from green to grey, becoming a wizened hag slumped across an old nag. Then, with surprising strength, she pulled Thomas up behind her on the horse and soon they were riding together into the deep woods. Eventually, Thomas saw three paths ahead of them, stretching into the distance: the left one was wide and gentle; the right one was steep and craggy; the third was winding and green, banked by purple heather and golden gorse. As he pointed to this route, she smiled playfully. 'That way leads to Faerie – where I am queen and few mortals have ever seen.'

The journey was filled with wonder for Thomas, for Faerie is like our own world, but wilder and brighter. They rode on until they came to a clearing, where a mansion of white marble stood gleaming in the moonlight. The doors were flung open and a host of servants gleefully greeted the rider who, as soon as she stepped over the threshold, immediately transformed again: from grey to green, from hag to Queen.

'You may stay here for three days, Thomas. Look and listen and enjoy, but let nothing pass your lips …'

Thomas was led into a magnificent ballroom, lit by flickering candles, where a table was laid with the finest food and drink. Guests arrived in leaf-green gowns and jackets and began to feast and drink, but Thomas kept his mouth tightly shut all the while. The following night, the tables were cleared and music began to play on fiddles and harps, with lilting tunes that Thomas had never heard the likes of before. On the third night the music increased in tempo, and the Queen and her guests spiralled and pirouetted in wild and wonderful dancing. Then, suddenly, the Queen waved her hand. The music immediately stopped, and the guests quickly bowed and left the room. Just a few moments later, Thomas was once more astride the milk-white mare, riding behind the Queen. The route they took out of Faerie was different to the way they came. They travelled through a dry, dusty desert, where a solitary fruit tree was growing, bearing a single, shiny apple. The Queen picked the apple and offered it to Thomas. 'This is the apple of truth. If you choose to eat it you will speak eloquently, but truthfully, at all times.'

He took the apple and ate it slowly as they travelled back to his own world. They stopped by the old hawthorn and there the Queen gave him another kiss – soft and light – without changing this time. Thomas's heart ached, with longing and loss.

'Farewell, Thomas. Look for another sign, when you least expect it, and you may return to my realm.'

With a flash of her green eyes and a swish of her horse's tail, she was gone. Thomas walked slowly through the bosky bluebells, which seemed somehow to have lost their lustre now. As he approached his manor house, villagers came out of their cottages to stand and stare. A maidservant, white with fright, told Thomas that he'd been missing for seven, long years. Everyone had thought he'd died in the wild woods, long ago.

His uncle had taken over the running of the estate during his absence and Thomas begged him to continue; he no longer had any interest in being laird of the land. Instead, he retreated to a cottage at the edge of the forest. There he lived alone among the trees, speaking eloquently but truthfully to any that came to visit. News spread of his way with words and many of the prophesies he made during that time eventually proved true. However, many found the truth-telling of Thomas the Rhymer hard to hear, and before long the stream of visitors dwindled.

Until one year, on the eve of May, with the hawthorn blossoming, Thomas saw a white deer, standing still and staring at him from the edge of the woods – he knew that this was the sign he'd been waiting for. As the deer disappeared, he was already following its footsteps through the forest, to the place where three paths diverge. And he knew which one to take ...

Bright Fires

In the Celtic calendar, with its underlying duality of a dark half and a light half of the year, Beltane marks the end of winter and the beginning of summer. Its liminality holds special significance: the cusp of the seasons, the transition from April into May, and the twilight period between day and night. It's a time when annual archetypal rivalries are played out: in one Celtic legend two opposing dragons fight for seasonal supremacy. Similarly, in Welsh mythology, two immortal heroes – Gwythyr ap Greidawl and Gwyn ap Nudd – battle each other on the eve of Calan Mai (1st May).

The word Beltane (sometimes spelled 'Beltaine') is generally thought to mean 'bright fire'. Bonfires are a focal point for all the Celtic celebrations at the opening of each season, but the flames hold special significance at Beltane. Fires imitate the heat of the sun and the sympathetic magic instilled in Beltane rituals encourage its warmth to rise through the season, as summer is kindled. In pastoral societies this was the time of year for grazing animals to be returned to green pastures. The flames, and smoke, of Beltane fires also played a role in both purifying and protecting precious livestock. The ashes from these outdoor bonfires held similarly protective powers when brought back to household hearths. As seen in the story of Thomas the Rhymer, dancing around a Beltane fire – clockwise, with the sun – invites blessings of fortune and fertility for the year ahead. Sometimes a lord and lady of May were chosen to leap through the flames of a fire, as an echo of symbolic 'sacrifice'. In some parts of Britain and Ireland the ritual flames have been nurtured over the years, and many more have been rekindled in modern-day seasonal celebrations, such as the renowned Beltane Fire Society in Edinburgh. For many of us, the bright fires of Beltane continue to bring a sense of 'wildness' into everyday lives, at a time when the natural world itself is rearing up in rampant growth and the Green Man is arising again.

Bringing in the May

The woodland bower is white with flower and green is every tree.

Just as Beltane fires light up our lives on the eve of May, so bringing nature's greenery and flowers into our homes on May Day symbolises and celebrates the renewal of life. Early in the morning is the traditional time to go into the woods and gather branches and blossoms from nature's refurnished bounty, then place them around our houses. It's an outward expression of an auspicious moment in the seasonal cycle, marking the start of the brightest and warmest quarter of the year: from May Day until Lammas. It's also a tangible method of re-engagement with nature after the dark days of winter. A posy of bright flowers on the table and green boughs around the doorway allows nature back into our homes, just as we feel inspired to step out into the wild world once more.

Hawthorn, also known as the May tree, begins to blossom at this time of year, and in the Old Calendar (see Introduction) its flowering would have more fully coincided with May Day festivities. It is a key cultural component of this month's many merry traditions, holding associations of frothing fertility and mischievous fairies. The rhyme 'here we go gathering nuts in May' originally derives from 'knots' of May – i.e., sprigs of hawthorn blossom. In Ireland it is often called whitethorn due to its creamy white flowers, and H.E. Bates poetically referred to the blossom as 'the risen cream of all the milkiness of May-time'. According to the folklore, May is the only time of year when it is acceptable to bring hawthorn into the house; otherwise it's associated with death and ill fortune. Sycamore, gorse, hazel, rowan and birch are also widely used for May-time greenery, reflecting local habitats and cultural traditions. Another seasonal splash of colour is added by the bright yellow of marsh marigolds at this time of year, as indicated by their folk names – May flower and May blobs.

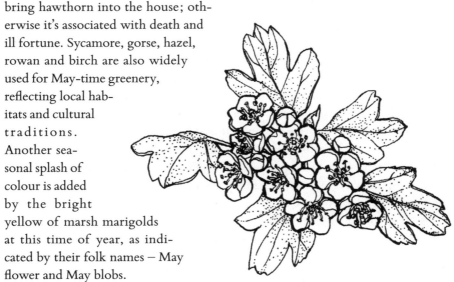

The May Tree

On Old Tom's farm there was a certain field, with a certain tree. A hawthorn tree – the tree of fairies and fertility and all the merriness of May. The tree grew in the middle of the field, causing quite an obstacle when it came to cutting the hay. But neither Old Tom, nor his father before him, would ever dream of felling a May tree – for fear of offending the fairies. But there was one thing that still bothered him about the tree: it never, ever produced flowers in springtime. Every year, at the beginning of May, he'd stand staring at the tree, as if willing it to burst into blossom. But it never did. And staring at trees was considered agriculturally reprehensible when there was plenty of work to be done on the farm. For several years, farm life was busy for Old Tom, as the well-tended land turned a tidy profit. But – as all farmers know – the tides of fortune ebb and flow, flow and ebb.

Soon the rent on his tenant farm was rocketing skywards, just as agricultural prices were tumbling. Good with his hands, but not with finances, Old Tom struggled to make ends meet. Drowning his sorrows, he started drinking more and was often late home to bed after a long night in the pub. On the way home he would often see the silhouette of the hawthorn tree that never bore blossom and soon it began to epitomise for Old Tom all the faults and failings of his farm. One night, at the end of a poor harvest, he found himself once more drinking hard with his hard-working friends, complaining about the hard times. It was late when he stumbled out of the pub, with the Harvest Moon hanging in the sky: cold and mocking. By the time he reached home, he was in a foul mood, vexing about the barren tree. He decided there and then that if it didn't blossom next year he would chop it down, regardless of the fairies. With that, he collapsed on to his bed with his boots on.

What Old Tom didn't know, was at the other end of the village there was a couple living in a little farm cottage, who for many years had been trying to have a baby – without success. Recently an elderly neighbour had passed on some traditional advice: that to conceive a child they should make love beneath the branches of a hawthorn tree, the fairy tree. So, the very night Tom was stumbling home from the pub, the couple picked their way along moonlit lanes then across dew-laden grass, until they reached his old tree. There, in the soft darkness, they took off their clothes and lay in each other's arms.

Well, sad to say, that winter was long, and harsh, and hard for Old Tom. But eventually, as it always does, spring came around once more: the wild world exploded into green growth and his spirits lifted a little. He worked hard fixing the fences around the farm, ready for the livestock to be returned to the fields.

It wasn't until the first day of May that he found himself in a certain field, with a certain tree. Suddenly he stopped to stare, a smile spreading across his weather-worn face, and tears welling in his eyes. Right in front of him, the May tree was covered in blossom – a shower of creamy flowers, that filled the air with their unmistakeable perfume.

That year for the first time in a long time, Old Tom went to the village May Day fair – greeting farming friends with a cheery wave and asking everyone if they'd seen his flowering hawthorn tree. At that same fair, there was a couple walking happily hand in hand. He had a broad smile on his face and she had broad bump across her belly. Sure enough, the very next month, the woman gave birth to a little girl – with lips as red as berries and skin as creamy white as hawthorn blossom. And, in honour of the blossoming tree, they called her May.

May Day, May Day

I like to rise when the sun she rises, early in the morning.

Greeting the rising sun early on May Morning is a long-standing and enduring magical moment in the cycle of the seasons – heralding the start of the light half of the year. Seeing the first rays of golden light breaking the dark horizon, just as the first blackbird sings in the valley below, is well worth getting up early for. As with many modern revivals of seasonal celebrations, these sunrise gatherings are often accompanied by local morris teams – dancing on a hill top (whatever the weather), then rolling down to the pub to drink in the atmosphere and sing May Day carols. At Cerne Abbas, in Dorset, the daybreak dancing takes place on Giant Hill, with the hulky chalk figure himself given a generous libation of ale from the local brewery.

In Cornwall, two well-known annual events celebrate May-time fertility through ritual folk dances: the 'Obby 'Oss in Padstow and Helston Flora Day, which are both preceded by decorating the towns in boughs of green and bowers of flowers. Not far away in Somerset, Minehead also has its own hobby horse, which rides out on May Day. In other places, flowery garlands are proudly paraded through the village, such as Abbotsbury Garland Day in Dorset, which takes place around Old May Day (13th May). The flowery bowers were originally offered as blessings to villagers' households (in exchange for generous giving) and then taken down to the sea for a blessing on the opening of the fisheries. Such thriving May Day celebrations, and many others in all their vibrant variety, are still valued, not only as seasonal markers, but in uniting the whole local community again outdoors.

> Where are the maidens that here now should sing?
> For summer is a-come unto day,
> They are in the meadows the flowers gathering,
> In the merry morning of May.

It's likely that maypoles originated as green boughs brought in from the woods, perhaps as ancient symbols of the World Tree (traditionally an ash) that holds the universe together in Norse mythology. They have become a popular focal point of many May Day celebrations, with coloured ribbons and interweaving style of dancing adopted in the nineteenth century. May Day is one of the main outings of the year for morris dancing sides, re-engaging with an older, wilder side of May Day festivities. Similarly, mummers' plays that are performed at this time of year often depict rebellious spirits of the wildwood, notably Robin Hood, whose marriage to Maid Marian also embodies the fertility of the season.

The May tradition of flaunting flowers and foliage has become transposed into an archetypal anthropomorphic form: the Green Man. His face – usually a striking composite of human and vegetative features – looms large in medieval imagery, including (ironically, perhaps) many Christian churches. Jack-in-the-Green, a walking, dancing representation of the Green Man, is most commonly seen in cities and towns; perhaps due to its association with chimney sweeps, who took the opportunity to raise money at a time when their work was dying down. In recent times, Jack-in-the-Greens have been enthusiastically revived in many places, including London, Bristol and Rochester, bringing nature-based revelry into urban locations where many people live and work. Alongside morris dancers and mummers' plays, they incorporate and reinterpret the Beltane theme of ushering in summer, as Old Man Winter is driven away by the growing powers of the Green Man.

The Darling Buds of May

As well as 'bringing in the May', there's both inspiration and opportunity for us to go outside to sense and savour the floweriness of May. The Romans celebrated the five-day festival of Floralia between 28th April and 2nd May, in honour of the fertility goddess Flora, who was venerated as the patron and protector of flowers. The month itself is named after Maia, a closely related Greek goddess of renewal. Beltane and May Day festivals have long been associated with flamboyant expressions of passion and fertility, in both natural and human worlds. Love is in the air, or at least lust, as this month is infamous for illicit liaisons:

> Married in May and churched in green,
> Both bride and groom won't long be seen.

Sex is also bursting out on the branches. After the green mist of April, a white flowery mantle is draped across woodlands and hedges in May, offering the opportunity to stop and enjoy the magical moment of spring flourishing into summer. Each year a tide of blossom stretches out from early April to late May on blackthorn, plum, damson, cherry, hawthorn, apple and elder trees (plus non-fruiting species such as rowan and hazel), gracing the landscape with pastel petals and heavenly scents. Our long love affair with blossom is highlighted by English being one of the few languages with its own specific word for 'tree-flowers' and in recent years the Japanese tradition of 'blossom-bathing' has caught our imagination at this time of year. Frothing cow parsley – also known as lady's lace, fairy lace or Queen Anne's lace – adds its own performance to this festival of floweriness. In natural synchrony, the symphony of early morning birdsong reaches its climax, as celebrated by International Dawn Chorus Day, held on the first Sunday of May. Time to stop and take it all in, before we get whisked away ...

Away with the Fairies

Bluebells form a swelling sea of blue under the emerging leaf canopy in May; especially intense within luminous, lime-green beechwoods. Their sight and smell are often dreamlike and otherworldly, and bluebells have long been associated with the fairies. In the tale of Thomas the Rhymer, his encounter with the Fairy Queen is precipitated by the presence of bluebells. It is said they 'ring' to call the Little People together for their revels in the woods, but for humans to hear that sound spells death or abduction into Faerie – not always a pleasant place for mortals. A garland of bluebells can compel the wearer to speak the truth, echoing the eventual fate of Thomas.

Fairies are believed to choose lone hawthorn trees as focal points for their May Eve revelries and as such are considered sacrosanct. In Ireland, in particular, there are many dark tales detailing the gruesome comeuppances of those who dare to interfere with a fairy bush. By contrast, offerings of food and drink left under their blossoming branches invite a blessing from the Little People. Thorns growing beside sacred wells are, to this day, decorated with colourful ribbons and rags, as a propitious ritual. In other folklore, if you prick a finger on a thorn, you'll fall into an enchanted asleep – the Icelandic word for hawthorn is 'sleep-thorn' and the spindle that pricked Sleeping Beauty in the fairy tale was made from hawthorn wood. Conversely, branches of hawthorn brought into the home at this time of year can also act as protection against being taken away by the fairies, especially in the case of 'changelings' (see August).

Both bluebells and hawthorn portend that the opening of May is a ripe time for encounters with the Others, including the Fairy Queen herself – as portrayed in *A Midsummers Night's Dream* (which, despite the title, takes place on May Eve). Thomas the Rhymer is unusual in wanting to re-enter Faerie, where few would dare to go, and even fewer return. In the *Ballad of Tam Lin*, a distinctly darker Scottish fairy tale, the central character is only able to wrest himself free from the powerful enchantments of the Fairy Queen through the determination of a young woman who truly loves him. In Welsh legend, there is a fairy island on Llyn Cwm Llwch, which mortals may visit once a year on May Day. But removing anything is strictly forbidden – one man who broke the taboo by taking an apple, ending up losing his mind.

The Milkiness of May

Awake, ye pretty maids, awake, refreshed from drowsy dream,
And haste unto dairy house to fetch a dish of cream.

The Anglo-Saxon name for May was Thrimilce, meaning the 'month of three milkings', reflecting the prolific milk production once grazing animals were returned to summer pastures with its lush spring growth.

Similarly, in the Anglo-Saxon lunar calendar, the name for a full moon in May is Milk Moon. New season milk was once so precious that milk-snatching witches and fairies were greatly feared; particularly on May Day eve, which was formerly the date of Mischief Night before it switched to Halloween. May-flowering plants, namely hawthorn, rowan and marsh marigold, were commonly used deterrents against supernatural dairy raids.

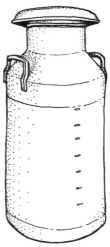

Throughout medieval times, May was also widely celebrated as the time of year when fresh dairy produce was welcomed back by consumers and customers. Milk maids literally made a song and a dance out of it, and were often accompanied by Jack-in-the-Greens (see above). Merry milk maids, along with ancient fertility goddesses, were perhaps the precursors of more modern May Queens – the feminine figureheads that often grace local May Day celebrations, wearing milk white dresses and flowery crowns.

Flavour of the Month

May Wine

Plants encountered as children can sometimes help identify those we might want to use later in adulthood. The bedstraw family contains a playful plant that you might well remember, which devilishly clings to clothes like Velcro. Sticky Willy, aka cleavers or goosegrass, is closely related to the vital ingredient in this recipe: sweet woodruff. This lower-lying and scented species is found in the woods. It has six to nine smooth, pointed green leaves extending from the square stem in whorls, with four-petalled white flowers. When crushed, it has the scent of fresh hay, but when drying has notes of cardamom, cinnamon and vanilla.

When you happen upon a bounty of wild herbs, there are a couple of great ways to enhance and preserve their unique flavour. Here we use gentle heat to convert the natural flavour compound, coumarin.

Two bottles of low-acidity, lightly sweet wine: Moselle and Riesling are the classically used grape styles but natively grown Bacchus is perfect for this drink.

15–20 spurs of sweet woodruff. These should be dried soon after collecting to ensure the coumarin doesn't convert to dicoumarol, which is toxic in large quantities (much more than used here).

– About four or five days ahead, bring home freshly foraged sweet woodruff and pre-heat an oven to 130–140°C; your sense of smell will guide timing rather than exact temperatures.
– Place the herbs on trays and into the heat. Usually, within five to seven minutes, the scent of vanilla and cardamom will flood the air.
– Open the wines and pour off a little, then quickly transfer these warm, dry spurs with their alluring odour into the wine. After a bit of prodding, re-corking and a subtle shake, store the bottles laid down in the fridge.

This stunning summer tipple, lengthened with soda, is the perfect pairing to sugar-steeped early strawberries. Ask friends to speculate which foraged ingredient is in the wine. Then ask them: 'What's that stuck to your back?'

Franken's Frosts

Although in folklore May is seen as the start of summer, it is not unknown for late frosts during the month to play havoc with farmers and growers. According to local legend, there was once a brewer of beer in Devon called Franken, who was increasingly jealous of a neighbouring cider-maker's popularity with the drinking population. So, one night in May, the Devil himself appeared and offered to help Franken by summoning three nights of frost to kill the apple blossom and foil the cider-maker's production. Since then, 19th to 21st May are now known as St Franken's Days in the Culmstock area of Devon, and every year there's a seasonal struggle to determine whether it will be a year of cider or beer drinking!

Beating the Bounds

In the church calendar, Rogationtide falls on the three days preceding Ascension Day – itself forty days after Easter, so it usually begins in May. The word derives from the Latin *rogare,* meaning 'to ask for'. During Saxon times, when physical maps were rare, this annual occasion developed into a custom called 'beating the bounds': a ritual perambulation of the parish perimeter to mark the territory and ask for a blessing on the fields and farmland within its boundaries. Traditionally, parishioners would use switches of green branches to actually beat the ground, or key features such as trees, as they recognised familiar places along the route. Beating the bounds has survived, or been revived, as a civic ceremony in many places around the UK; varying greatly in distance, duration and frequency. For instance, at Bodmin in Cornwall, the event comprises an invigorating 18-mile walk; although it only takes place every five years.

Tree Cheers

The end of May produces a final flourish of festivity, with three tree-related traditions. The 29th May is commonly known as Oak Apple Day, commemorating King Charles II hiding in an oak tree. Following the restoration of the monarchy in 1660, royalist followers would wear a sprig of oak leaves (often with an oak apple gall) on this day. Anyone failing to wear one was liable to be nipped, hence its alternative name of Pinch Bottom Day! In the Shropshire village of Aston-on-Clun, a black poplar, the Bride Tree, is the focus of a locally loved celebration on the same date, called Arbor Day. Flags are placed in the tree's branches alongside a costumed parade, morris dancing and general May merriness. Finally, the villagers of Great Wishford, in Wiltshire, rise early on the morning of 29th May every year to gather leafy boughs, of oak and hazel, from Grovely Woods. The tradition is seen as both a celebration of incoming summer and an assertion of ancient commoners' rights to collect firewood. The villagers then bring the greenery into Salisbury Cathedral, 6 miles away, declaring, 'Grovely, Grovely, All Grovely!'

Old Roots, New Shoots

PAROCHIAL MATTERS

The combination of returning warmth and flowery fertility in the wild world provides an ongoing instinctive impulse for us to make merry in May. As well as 'bringing in the May', it's a great time of year for bringing people together outdoors; with two bank holidays at either end of the month (in England) extending the festive opportunities. May Day itself is an ongoing tradition, with a rich and colourful palette of possibilities; to be celebrated in our own places, in our own ways. Since the late nineteenth century, 1st May has also been adopted as the date for International Workers' Day, channelling the rebellious spirit of the season and celebrating acts of collective solidarity, including standing up for public access to the countryside.

The playful plurality of Maytime celebrations allows us to embrace the idea of 'local distinctiveness', as championed by environmental arts charity Common Ground over many years. Drawing on the tradition of beating the bounds, their parish maps project facilitates communities to proactively take stock of their local patch: collaboratively charting the places, features and wildlife that are most valued within the parish. As such, it provides an enjoyable, accessible opportunity for people who live in the same area to get together annually and reacquaint themselves with their wider neighbourhood, at a time of year when the outdoors is at its showy best. Regardless of who owns the land, such communal gatherings can help engender a sense of belonging – to a place and its people – by celebrating the parochial, the commonplace and the everyday. May, the force, be with you!

6

June

The bonny month of June is crowned with the sweet scarlet rose;
The groves and meadows all around with flowery pleasure flows.

Dawn and Dusk

In the beginning, after creating the cosmos, the Sky God needed help with the ordering of the heavens and managing the movements of its celestial bodies. So, he came down to Earth and chose two suitable servants; a young man and a young woman. In return for their divine duties, he offered them both immortality and eternal youth.

The young man was named Dusk and the Sky God entrusted him with the setting of the sun. 'Each evening you must douse its flames and wrap it in a thick blanket of darkness, then hide it well so that no harm should come to the sun.'

The young woman was called Dawn and the Sky God entrusted her with the rising of the sun. 'Each morning you must wake the sun, re-ignite its flames and send it soaring out across the sky by day.'

Dawn and Dusk willingly agreed to their tasks and performed their heavenly roles with dutiful diligence. Each evening and morning, the sun was cradled and kindled in turn, with the times varying through the seasons, as ordained by the Sky God himself. Over the months and years, spinning and spanning into centuries, Dusk and Dawn continued their tasks; mostly in isolation from each other. But in the high summer months, when the time and distance between the two of them was short, the young man and woman would gaze at each other across the star-crossed sky. Slowly, but surely, they fell in love. As their passion peaked, they could no longer contain their desire for each other and pleaded with the Sky God to allow them to be together.

The Sky God smiled indulgently, then replied, 'Your love deserves to be honoured, so I offer you a choice. You may leave your tasks in the heavens and return to Earth where you may live, and love, together for the rest of your lives – but only for the normal time span of human life. Or continue in your heavenly duties and I will arrange for you to be together, freely and fully, for one night each year – at midsummer. Then, your lives will continue to stretch on for all eternity. Which will you choose?'

They weighed both options, but chose the latter. In gratitude the Sky God arranged for that one night of the year – summer solstice – to be the most beautiful: the stars tweaked into twinkling perfection; the air made soft and warm and the Earth furnished with flowers and their heavenly scents. That first Midsummer's Night, between Dusk and Dawn, was like a dream – short, but certainly sweet. Early in the morning, as the sun rose, it blushed bright red at the sight of those two young, naked lovers. As it does every year when they meet together at summer solstice ...

Turning Full Circle

The wheel of the solar year swings around to its highest point at the summer solstice, usually on either 20th or 21st June, when the Northern Hemisphere is tilted closest towards the sun. The word solstice derives from the Latin *sol* (sun) and *sistere* (to stand still), as the sun seems to pause in its path across the seasonal sky before changing direction. For a few days, either side of the solstice, sunrise and sunset occur at similar times; as they mark the longest days of the year with just a few hours between dusk and dawn. It's an auspicious time of year, when the power of the fiery sun is paramount, and has been eagerly anticipated since the dawn of time. Stone circles and other ancient monuments across northern Europe are aligned with the rising sun at summer solstice, such as Stonehenge in England and Newgrange in Ireland.

Following Beltane's flames at the inception of summer, ceremonial bonfires mirror the fullness of the sun's powers and celebrate the longer days. Leaping over the flames of bonfires was considered lucky at this time, to propitiate a good harvest, with the elevation of the jump foretelling the height of that year's crops. Other solstice customs included sending a burning, wooden wheel spinning down a hill, representing the sun's journey through the year, and guided by people with sticks on its way down, before being quenched in a river at the bottom. Poignantly, and importantly, the moment of the sun's seasonal peak also marks the very beginning of its descent and slow demise towards the winter solstice in December. It has long been held as a sensitive seasonal moment filled with both promise and compromise – as highlighted in the Dawn and Dusk story.

St John's Fires

The sun shines on the righteous.

Pagan celebrations for summer solstice have been adapted and adopted within the Christian calendar as the feast day of St John the Baptist, held on 24th June. This, in turn, was eventually subsumed back into the popular cycle of seasonal festivities, hence Midsummer's Day is celebrated a few days after the summer solstice itself. Late June – from St John's Day through to St Peter's Day on 29th June – was enjoyed as an extended period of midsummer merrymaking, reflecting the fact that these few days are almost equally light and long. St John's Eve continued the old tradition of midsummer fires, referring to them as 'wake fires' – i.e. staying awake to keep vigil (for St John, in this case). In medieval times, a 'wake' became an opportunity for, even synonymous with, a festive communal party (see August). St John's fires are still lit religiously every year in some parts of Britain and, especially, Ireland. In recent years, a fiery celebration of midsummer has been re-ignited in Penzance, where the vibrant festival of Golowan brings the town to life. The town's patron is St John, with the name of the event itself deriving from the Cornish for the saint: Gol Jowan. This modern-day community festival has grown steadily as a colourful, living tradition, now comprising more than a week and combining community arts with older midsummer folklore.

The heat and smoke of St John's fires were also seen as a means of purification; to protect land and livestock from both disease and devilry. Defences against dark forces, especially witches, were commonplace at this time of year: in the Cornish villages of Callington and St Cleer, midsummer fires, topped by broomsticks, are referred to as 'Banishing the Witches'. St John also has his own plant named after him – St John's wort – which is also known as 'chase Devil' because of its believed properties for supernatural protection. It was often hung over doorways and in barns, as well as woven into garlands, after being picked at midsummer:

> St John's wort doth charm all witches away,
> If gathered at midnight on the saint's holy day.
> Any devils and witches have no power to harm
> Those that gather the plant for a charm.

There is also a plant (a type of stonecrop) called 'midsummer men', which was once gathered on Midsummer's Eve by young men and placed in cracks around the doors of their sweethearts. The plant is capable of staying alive for a long time after being picked and the direction its leaves grew was seen as an augury for the fate of the love match.

Flower Power

> Married in the month of roses, June,
> Life will be one long honeymoon.

The month of June takes its name from the Roman goddess Juno, the wife of Jupiter and presiding over marriage, love and childbirth. According to legend, she gave birth to Mars after being touched by a flower given to her by fellow goddess Flora. Juno was also venerated as the deity of vitality and renewal (giving rise to the word 'rejuvenation'), reflecting the vibrant vegetation and the flowery fields at midsummer. Her month of June has long been a popular month to get married, after May's more frivolous affairs. The Anglo-Saxon name for a full moon in June is Flower Moon, appearing at a time of year when the air is increasingly filled with floral scents. Other Anglo-Saxon names for the month are Seramonath, meaning 'dry month', and Lida, which translates as gentle or mild, referring to the weather conditions around midsummer.

The gentle warmth and long days in June give rise to a flush of first flowering for many plants, such as honeysuckle, foxglove, cranesbills and roses of various kinds. Wildflower meadows, nationally rare but slowly reviving in many parts of the UK, now reach their peak of petalled perfection. Meadow specialists, such as cornflower, knapweed, bird's foot trefoil and yellow rattle, provide both colourful names and vibrant views. Ox-eye daisy, another key component of wildflower meadows, has alternative folk names of midsummer daisy and thunder daisy, reflecting the timing of its flowering season.

The Midsummer Rose

Sally was young and in love. Her sweetheart was a handsome farm labourer called Will – honest and hard-working, but not considered a suitable suitor by her well-to-do Devon family. 'You'll change your mind, or he'll change his. Wait 'til you're older, someone better will come along,' they said, thinking she'd soon fall out of love.

But Sally would not be swayed in her affections for Will, and instead looked for a way to prove her fidelity. The only person who truly listened to Sally was her old grandmother, who lived in the neighbouring village of Berry Pomeroy. Whilst visiting her stone cottage one bright June morning – Midsummer's Day itself – she offered Sally a possible solution. At midday, her grandmother told her to go and pick one of the blossoming white roses from the front garden. Then she gave Sally instructions: 'Wrap the rose in tissue and place it carefully in the pages of your father's old Bible at home. Leave it there, untouched, until Christmas Day. Then, when you wear a still-fresh rose to church, everyone will see the truth of your blossoming love.'

Sally willingly, and gratefully, followed her grandmother's advice – then waited. It was a long six months from midsummer to midwinter. Every day, Sally was tempted to reach up to the high shelf and open the Bible; but she kept faith in her grandmother's words. At long last, Christmas morning came, cold and clear, with a hard frost nipping the air. Sally made an excuse to walk by herself to church and arrived wearing the white rose, as fresh as the midsummer's day when it was picked. Everyone, including her family, admired and remarked on the miracle of a rose in winter, and they also clearly saw Sally's enduring love for Will. She gave the rose to Will that day. And another six months later they were happily married in the same church, on Midsummer's Day, just as the white roses in her grandmother's garden were blossoming once more.

A Rose by Any Other Name

Roses, both wild and cultivated, are among the most conspicuous and admired flowers to bloom in June. If picked on Midsummer's Eve, roses can allegedly stay fresh until Midwinter's Day (as the previous folk tale illustrates). Roses were once used as tokens for nominal rents, traditionally paid on Midsummer's Day as one of the four quarter days of the year. Two examples of 'rose rent' traditions survive – in London and Leicester. The flower emblem of England is a Tudor rose, combining (through royal marriage) the red rose of Lancaster and the white rose of York. Several English villages, especially in Lancashire, continue a tradition of crowning a rose queen each year, usually as part of a local summer fête or pageant.

Roses are associated with the Greek goddess of love, Aphrodite, and in folklore symbolise both passion and pain. In several folk tales the sharp consequences of desire are often signified through the briars surrounding its flowers; there is no rose without a thorn. In one old legend, a nightingale was once so enamoured with a white rose that he pressed his breast against the thorns, staining the petals red with his dying blood. Late June is certainly the time of year when the fervent singing of nightingales begins to die down. The dog rose, with pretty, pale pink flowers despite its unflattering name, is the most commonly encountered species in the wild; seen scrambling along many an old hedgerow. It is also the answer to a delightfully botanically precise riddle:

> On a summer's day, in sultry weather
> Five Brethren were born together.
> Two had beards and two had none
> And the other had but half a one.

Apparently, 'Brethren' refers to the five sepals beneath the flowers, and whether or not they have hairy edges.

Zebedee and Zachary

Once there were, and I reckon there still are, two old neighbours in Dorset. The two men each had a piece of land, one beside the other. But even though they were born and brought up in the same place, in character they were as different as chalk and cheese. The first man was called Zebedee, easy-going and laid-back, who only worked as much as was needed – spending the rest of his time in sport and play. He savoured the joys of each season and was never happier than with a glass of cider in his hand and a folk song on his tongue. The second man was called Zachary and he was the exact opposite: hard-nosed, stony-faced and tight-fisted. He wouldn't waste his precious time on drinking and dancing; he'd rather be making money. He often scorned and sneered at his neighbour Zebedee's wild and wanton ways.

One night, on Midsummer's Eve, Zebedee was out late, after singing songs and sipping at a friend's cider barn. It was well into the early hours when he found himself stumbling home, passing by the bulky shadows of Winterbourne Abbas stone circle. Suddenly, an eerie scraping sound filled the still night air, raising the hairs on the back of Zebedee's neck. Turning towards the megaliths, he watched with wide, cidery eyes as two of the standing stones began to wriggle up and out of their earth-bound sockets. Slowly, with a weird, slumping motion, they began to shuffle along the ground, down towards a nearby stream. There they bent down, with a creak and a crack, and began to drink the trickling water with unmistakable gulps and slurps. For a while, Zebedee was spellbound, but then ran home like a hunted hare to sleep off the strangeness of the night.

But the next day the sights and sounds he'd witnessed were still vivid in his head. Needing to tell someone, he went to see his neighbour, Zachary. How he laughed – loud and long – when he heard Zebedee's zany story of standing stones walking down to the stream. 'You must have had a proper dose of cider last night! I've never heard so much rubbish in all my life!'

'But it's true,' retorted Zebedee. 'My father, and his old man before him, always said that those stones come alive at midsummer. Now I've seen it with me own eyes! Them are sacred stones, I tell yer.'

'Listen to me, the only thing that's sacred is money. And the only thing those old stones are good for is building material. Watch and I'll prove that you're just as daft as your father ever was ...'

So, the following week Zachary arranged for work horses and labourers to painstakingly dig up, and drag away, four of the standing stones from Winterbourne Abbas circle. He used them as cornerstones for building a new barn, with timber sides and a thatched roof. When it was finished, he stood back to admire the construction – a visible symbol of his material success.

The seasons continued to cycle round, until once more it was the eve of Midsummer's Day. As usual, Zebedee was making merry with songs, cider and stories to celebrate the longest day. Zachary, however, was already tucked up for the night. But, in the early hours of the morning, he was rudely awakened by a loud, cracking sound that made him sit bolt upright in bed, wide awake. Looking through the window he could see his beloved barn shuddering and shaking in the moonlight. Pulling on his clothes, Zachary went outside and watched in astonishment as the old stones began to wrench themselves out of position. He rushed forward, vainly trying to save his barn, but now that the cornerstones were out of place, the whole building came tumbling down. The large wooden crossbeam crashed down, striking Zachary dead. Meanwhile, keeping their annual appointment, the four stones steadily made their way down to the stream for a drink.

As for Zebedee, he lived a long and leisurely life, merrily celebrating the seasons. He never did see the stones moving again, but sometimes, on Midsummer's Eve, he heard strange, scraping sounds …

Rolling Stones

One of the most enduring, and alluring, of British myths is that of standing stones becoming magically animated on Midsummer's Eve. In most cases, they slowly manoeuvre themselves down to a local stream for a 'drink' at midnight, then back to their prehistoric positions by dawn. It's considered wise for humans to steer clear of such powerful elemental forces at such times of year, as the story above illustrates. In other local legends, the Devil is said to appear if you count the same number of stones while circumnavigating an ancient stone circle three times. Several stone circles, such as Stanton Drew in Somerset, are said to originate from summertime wedding guests dancing all night to the Devil's fiddle tunes, before being turned into stone as daylight breaks on the morning of the Sabbath.

The Rollright Stones in Oxfordshire have their own stirring story. Long ago, a foreign warlord arrived in England at the head of an invading army, but was confronted by an old hedge witch. She prophesied that he would only become King if he could see the neighbouring village of Long Compton after seven strides up the slope. The King confidently marched uphill, but on his seventh stride the ground supernaturally rose up in front of him, so he wasn't able to see the village beyond. In that moment, the witch called out, 'Rise up, stick and stand still, stone, For King of England thou shalt be none.' The King and his nearby knights were immediately turned into four tall standing stones (known as the Whispering Knights), while down below his whole army was simultaneously petrified into a stone circle. The witch herself then transformed herself into an elder tree, rooted to the ground nearby.

Elder Mother

Elder trees come into blossom by early June. Their frothy, white flowers, full of fragrance and abuzz with nectaring insects, are among the unmistakable sights and smells of high summer. They taste delicious too: fried in a batter as fritters, bottled as elderflower cordial or fermented into elderflower champagne. The name 'elder' is thought to come from the Old English word *aeld*, meaning fire, as its hollow stems were used to blow air into embers and rekindle the flames. These days they are a popular practical material in forest schools for whittling into necklaces, pencils and whistles. The leafy branches of elder trees were once hung from doorways as protection against evil spirits, as well as to keep flies away from barns and cowsheds.

In northern European folklore, the spirit of the tree elder is called Hyldemoer (Elder Mother), with a distinctly bittersweet personality: cruel if crossed, but generous to those she favours. Many healing or health-giving qualities have been ascribed to different parts of elder trees in traditional remedies. In the Rollright Stones legend, the elder witch clearly has as protective role, keeping the kingdom safe from invading powers. On the darker side, malicious elder witches are believed to haunt the woods in autumn (see September). Judas himself is said to have hanged himself from an elder tree after betraying Jesus, adding to its sinister associations. It's sometimes referred to as 'God's Stinking Tree', due to its overripe flowers smelling a bit like cat's urine!

Flavour of the Month

Elderflower Fritters with
Wild Strawberry Granola and Gooseberry Fool

Asking permission of the elder tree feels significant, knowing that it'll provide year-round its flowers, fruits and seeds, and even be a host to the easily identifiable jelly ear fungus. June means elderflower champagne, and we never fail to make any. Few people realise that the scented creamy white flowers also make great eating. All preparations of elderflower must employ heat or fermentation to denature any toxins. Along with the intensely flavoured wild strawberry and gooseberry, it can create a celebratory pudding that sings 'summer is here!'

Prepare the wild strawberry granola and the gooseberry fool ahead.

FOR THE GRANOLA
Petite wild strawberries have a somewhat freeze-dried texture right off the plant and make a great addition to this lightly caramelised crunchy mix.

> 40g light olive oil
> 80g golden syrup
> 1 tsp vanilla extract
> ¼ tsp cinnamon
> ¼ tsp ground cardamom
> 160g oats
> 10g muscovado
> 30g caster sugar
> 1 cup, or thereabouts, of wild strawberries

– Preheat the oven to 200°C, then heat the olive oil, golden syrup, two sugars and vanilla in a pan until combined.
– Add the spices and oats and stir in well.
– Fold in the wild strawberries. Spread on a non-stick oven tray.
– Bake for five minutes, then turn the mix over with a non-stick spatula.
– Return to the oven in two-minute intervals, repeating until the blend begins to caramelise, which may take four turns.
– Cool the mixture before storing it in a sealed glass jar.

FOR THE FOOL

250g punnet of gooseberries
230ml Jersey cream
60g caster sugar

– Simmer the gooseberries with 30g of sugar for eight minutes and cool to room temperature.
– Whisk the unctuous thick Jersey cream to a satin consistency with the remaining sugar. Fold in the gooseberry sauce and refrigerate as needed.

FOR THE ELDERFLOWER FRITTERS

Oil for frying, oven pre-heated to 180°C
16 fresh (unwashed) elderflower blooms, checked for insects, with stalks removed
90g self-raising flour
30g cornflour
15g icing sugar
250ml chilled sparkling water
1 free-range egg white, beaten to soft peaks
25ml rose water

The batter is a take on tempura, but with the heady addition of rose water. We are looking to create a cold, light batter with lumps in, without overmixing the ingredients.

– Put the flour, cornflour, icing sugar and rose water in a bowl. Mix in the sparkling water, not particularly well, then leave to stand for an hour.
– Fold the beaten egg white into the batter.
– Dip a couple of heads at a time into the batter, lightly shake off excess and gently drop into the oil.
– Remove onto kitchen paper with a slotted spoon when lightly golden.
– Layer up the gooseberry fool in glasses with a good sprinkling of the wild strawberry granola in between.
– Serve with the warm elderflower fritters. Make sure you say thanks to your elders.

One Tree Hill

Once there was a small hill in Derbyshire where three birch trees grew – tall, green and graceful. The land belonged to an old farmer who'd lived and worked there the whole of his life. But he never spoke of owning the land, only caring for it while it was in his keeping. Once a year, on Midsummer's Day, he gathered posies of fresh flowers from the fields and hedges – colourful roses and poppies, sweet-smelling elderflowers and honeysuckle – and laid them on the roots of the trees, as a gift of gratitude. Sometimes, as he looked back at the hill in the evening, he thought he could see three green ladies dancing gently, with the flowers in their hair.

The old farmer had three grown sons. At the end of his time, he gathered them by his bedside with his final requests: to care for the land as he had done and to leave flowers for the 'green ladies' on Midsummer's Day. At first, the eldest son inherited the farm, but not his father's love of the land – to him it was just a means of making money. Fields were widened and hedgerows removed to increase productivity and profits. When he saw his youngest brother climbing the hill in late June with a posy of flowers he scoffed, 'That old superstition should've died with our father!' A few days later the eldest brother decided to fell one of the birch trees for timber to build new fences. All day he hacked away with his axe, but just as the tree began to fall, an unexpected gust of wind caught the branches. The tall birch came crashing down – killing the eldest son where he stood, axe still in hand.

Next the farm passed to the middle son. He was idle and arrogant – expecting to make an easy living from the land without doing any of the hard work. The farm quickly fell into rack and ruin, choked by weeds and covered in brambles and briars. He didn't even notice when his younger brother climbed the hill with flowers on Midsummer's Day. But as the weather turned cold, he needed firewood to keep warm, so climbed the hill to chop down one of the two remaining trees. Once more, just as the tree began to topple, a sudden gust blew it backwards – striking down the second son instantly.

Finally, the farm, including the hill with its one remaining tree, passed to the youngest son. Remembering his father's final wishes, he worked hard – tilling the land and tending the animals – and soon the farm was thriving and flourishing once more. Every year he continued to climb the hill on Midsummer's Morning to leave a posy of sweet summer flowers on the roots of the last birch. And each time, as he looked out in the gloaming at the end of the day, he thought he could see a single green lady dancing lightly, with flowers in her hair.

Tree's Company

Ellum he do grieve,
Oak he do hate,
Willow do walk,
If you travels late.

This striking folk saying, collected by Somerset folklorist Ruth Tongue, evokes a widespread belief that certain trees sometimes take on human attributes and abilities, especially under the influence of midsummer magic. A range of British folk tales about walking, talking trees reveal that (just like humans) they can be both good and bad in nature; dealing out either reward or revenge. One Derbyshire legend tells of an unwary traveller encountering a malevolent ash tree called Crooker. He is only saved from its evil intents by virtue of carrying a posy of St John's wort flowers, given to him by a local wise woman. According to a Scottish travellers' tale, an ancient oak called Old Croovie uproots himself to dance with young birch trees every hundred years, on Midsummer's Eve. The root hole Old Croovie leaves behind is said to contain buried treasure for anyone brave, or foolish, enough to try and take it.

The Royal Oak

Sing Oak, and Ash, and Thorn, good sirs,
(All of a Midsummer morn!)
Surely we sing of no little thing,
In Oak, and Ash, and Thorn!

Oak trees reach their fullness at midsummer, with wide crowns of green leaves efficiently soaking up the sun's peak energy; reflected in oak's excellence as firewood and charcoal. The synergy of tall oaks and summer seems synonymous with regal strength and royal power, which is still held within English idioms: hearts of oak, royal oak, as strong as an oak. There is a belief that fairies moved into old oak trees to hide when Christianity arrived, and still dance around their trees at certain times of year. The Irish word for oak is *duir*, translating as door, and oaks are often seen as portals to the otherworld in folk tales. The name druid is also related to this word, referring to 'oak wisdom'. In Celtic mythology, the two halves of the year are presided over by two archetypal figures: the Oak King and the Holly King. The Oak King rules the waxing year, born at winter solstice and reaching his full strength at the summer solstice in June. Crowns of oak leaves were also once worn by earthly rulers, as a symbol of victory in battle. However, like the sun itself, at summer solstice the Oak King gives way to the Holly King, who gains power through the waning year, reaching his peak powers in December. The fall of John the Baptist and the rise of Jesus are also said to echo the duality of the Oak King and the Holly King at midsummer.

Ferny Feeling

Since ferns have no flowers or seeds, as such, people have long wondered how they reproduce. The delicate, and difficult to see, spores are produced around midsummer, giving rise to a myriad of supernatural associations with ferns at this time of year. It is said that a covering of fern 'seeds' can render a person invisible, whether desired or not. Spending Midsummer's Eve outdoors in a place where ferns grow is a sure way to encounter one of the fairy folks. Their magical charms can lead to hidden treasure, or even reveal the secrets held within another person's heart. However, it's wise to tread carefully on the way home, as to stand on a 'fairy' fern can result in losing your way; endlessly wandering the woods, unseen ...

Old Roots, New Shoots

A MIDSUMMER NIGHT'S DREAM

Midsummer's Eve, or around then, is the perfect time to stay awake and savour the sweetness of a summer's night. The weather is (hopefully) clement and kind, and the air is filled with flowery scents ordained by the Sky God himself. It's a heaven-sent opportunity to stay up late, camp out or simply sleep under the stars, as Dawn and Dusk meet briefly and beautifully in the sky. Sunsets are slower and lower around summer solstice; and later for a few days afterwards. Many people, now, as well as in the past, gravitate to a stone circle, standing stone or other ancient monument on this night (but watch out for moving monoliths!). At Blackdown hill near Dorchester, for instance, the Dorset AONB recently commissioned a brand-new stone circle with apertures that align with sunrise and sunset at summer and winter solstices. Perhaps enjoy some stargazing, lying down on the earth and looking up at the sky, spotting the constellations and recalling their associated myths and legends – the starry stories. Alternatively, enjoy listening to the nocturnal sounds of wildlife in your local nature spots, such as nightjars with their strange and mesmerising churring sound, calling the seasons onwards …

7

July

In comes the jolly scythes-men,
To mow the meadow down,
With the good old leather bottle,
And the ale that is so brown.

All's Well

Once, in Derbyshire, there was an old woman who lived by herself in a little, stone cottage, with one room, one window and one door. She was a clean and tidy woman, who kept the earth floor and the fireplace well swept with her goose wing brush. The farmer, who owned the cottage, came by once in a while to collect the rent and leave a few provisions: turves of peat for the fire, fresh hay for her bed and a sack of oatmeal to make porridge. He was her only regular visitor, and was a gentle and generous man, if a little forgetful. Some weeks he forgot to visit altogether, but then again, he hardly ever remembered to collect the rent. The old woman's front garden was filled with a riot of summer-flowering plants, including hollyhocks and clematis in different colours. Just inside the front gate was a bubbling spring, covered by a large, flat rock, which flowed with cool, clear water throughout the year. So, altogether the old woman had everything she needed: a stone roof, four stout walls, a soft bed to sleep on and spring water to drink. 'How lucky I am!' she often said to herself. 'But I wouldn't mind a bit o' good company …'

One warm day in July, the farmer came riding by. In addition to his usual provisions, he'd also brought a little bowl of ripe, red raspberries from his allotment and a small gooseberry bush for her to plant in her own garden. The woman was delighted with the gifts, for she loved the sweetness of summer berries. She persuaded the farmer to stay a while, so leaning on the gatepost he shared the latest local news. By and by, they discussed the old squire having recently died and a young nephew taking over residence at the Manor House. The farmer related how, that very morning, all the servants had left because the new squire had refused to allow them to leave any food and drink for the 'Luck' (the household spirit who'd been there for generations). 'Dear me!' said the old woman, shaking her old, grey head solemnly. 'No good will come from losing your Luck …'

After the farmer had gone, the woman planted her gooseberry bush in the garden, giving it a sprinkling of water from the well. Then she set about making a pot of porridge to go with the raspberries, doubling the usual amounts of oats in the hope that a neighbour might join her to share a bowl full and a yarn. But no one came, so instead she left the other bowl by the fireplace, thinking of the 'Luck' turfed out of his ancestral home. That evening, after a long day of sultry summer weather, a thunderstorm rumbled overhead. The old woman lay awake in her bed listening to the sound of raindrops dancing on the roof. Then, in the middle of the night, she heard a strange, thin voice calling out in the dark:

> Oh dear, where can I go,
> In summer showers and winter snow?
> Oh dear, what will I do,
> Let me come in and stay with you …

In the morning, the old woman smiled to see the empty bowl. But then was astonished to find a stack of dry turves by the fire and a full sack of oatmeal on the kitchen table.

'Thank-you kindly whoever you are!' she shouted up the chimney, and from then on she happily set food and water by the fire – just for the Luck.

The next day, she heard the sound of squeaking wheels outside and through the window she saw a tinker running along at full tilt with his hand cart. She would have dearly liked to share a bit of conversation with the traveller, but he was in too much haste (having recently helped himself to a couple of rabbits from the squire's estate). The loaded cart bounced along with such a jolt that a little tin mug fell off the back. The woman picked it up admiringly, as the tinker disappeared down the road. 'How lucky I am! Everything I need and now a little tin mug to drink from …'

On the second day, another horse and cart came by – loaded high with newly cut rushes – and two sun-bronzed labourers strolling along with scythes across their broad shoulders. She hoped the men might tarry a while for a sip of well water, but they were keen to get home for their suppers. However, seeing how well she kept her cottage and garden, they unloaded a couple of armfuls of fresh rushes to cover her floor. Once spread out evenly, her house was even more neat and tidy than before. 'How lucky I am! Everything I need and now new rushes for my floor ...'

On the third day, a neighbour stopped at the gate to ask the old woman if she could spare some petals from the hollyhocks and honeysuckle growing in her garden. 'I need flowers for Well-dressing Day. But I see you have your own little well, so perhaps you'll be using them all yourself?'

'Oh goodness me, no!' she replied. 'My fingers are too old for picking petals and my eyes are too weak for making pretty pictures. Please, go ahead and help yourself – there's plenty of flowers there.'

Later that evening, in gratitude for the flowers, the neighbour came back with two freshly baked cakes. After eating one, the old woman left the other, and the tin mug filled with spring water, by the hearth. She went to bed early, imagining how lovely it would be to have her own well decorated with flowers. The next morning, she awoke to the smell of roses drifting in through the open window. Stepping out of the front door, she saw that the flat rock over her well was festooned with flowers – all arranged into a perfect pattern of multi-coloured petals. Some she recognised from her own garden, but others were clearly from cultivated roses – yellow, crimson and cream – that had somehow been translocated from the grand gardens of the Manor House.

'Such a beautifully decorated well, and in my own garden! 'Tis a shame I live so far from the village for others to come and see it.'

However, later that day, the farmer came to the old woman's cottage, with the well-dressing judges perched precariously on the back of his horse and cart. Stepping into her garden, they were amazed at the colourful design and intricate decoration of the well. After a short consultation, they declared her to be that year's worthy winner – with a prize of three silver coins. The four of them then spent the rest of the day happily sitting in her flowery garden, drinking freshly drawn spring-water from the well and chewing the cud 'til the cows came home. For the rest of that week, a steady stream of visitors came to visit her brightly dressed well and pay their regards to the old woman in her tidy little cottage. She was delighted, after all those years, to have a small moment of fame and fortune; but she didn't neglect the source of her good providence. She still remembered to leave a little something by the hearth for the Luck. So, in the evenings, sitting there by the fireside, she didn't feel lonely any more: 'How lucky I am! Everything I need and now a little company, as well!'

Rushing Around

Green grow the rashes-o, Green grow the rashes-o;
The sweetest hours that e'er I spent, Are spent among the lasses-o.

Robert Burns

Rushes are evergreen, long-stemmed plants that grow in dense clumps in damp habitats, such as floodplains and marshland – mostly in the cooler, wetter corners of Britain and Ireland. Being locally abundant and hard-wearing in nature, they were once commonly used as a floor covering, providing insulation and (relative) comfort when laid over hard, bare earth. In both domestic households and churches, floor rushes were regularly replenished – especially in summer when the plants reached a peak of growth and could be combined with other scented summer vegetation, such as yellow flag and meadowsweet. The act of bringing in new-cut rushes developed into a communal ritual, commonly called 'rush bearing', often with a focus on the village church on one particular date in the year, usually in July and August.

Although the need for rush flooring has long since passed, the ceremony of cutting and bearing rushes survived as a seasonally distinctive folk tradition within some local communities; particularly in the north-west of England. Rush-bearing events were often associated with regional summer holidays and provided a focus for friendly rivalry between local towns and villages keen to outdo each other in the decoration of their rush carts. Several Cumbrian villages still hold annual rush-bearing festivals, including Ambleside on the first weekend of July. In Saddleworth, on the Lancashire–Yorkshire border, the lively rush cart tradition has been celebrated for the last forty years, with a gravity-defying tower of rushes pulled by morris dancers. A villager is selected as the 'jockey', perched on top, and treated like local royalty with a steady supply of beer.

The supple strength of rushes also makes them valuable in a range of other traditional crafts – including ropes, seat mats and nets – and the absorbent pithy interior was once widely used as wicks in 'rush lights' (see the White Moth story) and even as fuses for explosives used by Cornish miners.

Ladies' bedstraw flowers and meadowsweet appear profusely along riverbanks in July and were used both in floor mats and in mattresses as well as an aromatic flavour in drinks (see this month's recipe). According to legend, its name originates from dried ladies' bedstraw being used as bedding material when the Virgin Mary gave birth. It's also known as bride of the meadow.

Make Hay While the Sun Shines

The Anglo-Saxon name for July was Meadmonath, meaning 'meadow month', and the designation for a full moon this month is Hay Moon, or sometimes Mead Moon. Providing the weather holds, this is the time when the hay meadows are cut, traditionally with scythes. An interest in scything, as both a countryside skill and an effective means of managing meadows for wildlife, has revived hugely recently. The popular Green Scythe Fair, held annually in summer at Muchelney on the Somerset Levels, includes a scything competition to test the mettle of the West Country's finest haymakers. It's highly energetic work and needful of a full stomach ...

The Hungry Mowers

Every summer, a Sussex farmer hired the same two seasonal workers to help mow the hay, as fodder for his livestock through the winter. Being strong in the arm and skilled with a scythe, he relied on these two men to cut the meadows as quickly as possible, before thundery rain could spoil the hay. In return for the work, they were paid both in cash and subsistence; including a meal in the farmhouse at the beginning and the end of the day.

One year, however, the farmer was dismayed to discover the men making sluggish progress with their scything. From the gateway, he heard them slowly chanting, 'Curds and whey, every day! Curds and whey, every day!' The old farmer went back to the farmhouse and asked his wife what she'd been giving them for breakfast. When he found out they'd had a meagre bowl of curds and whey, he told her to make sure they both received a hearty breakfast from then on.

Sure enough, the very next morning, he watched them swinging their scythes swiftly through the hayfield, their vigorous voices rising over the hedgerow, 'Ham 'n' eggs, mind yer legs! Ham 'n' eggs, mind yer legs!'

Well-Dressed

Springs and wells once provided vital freshwater for local communities; literally a source of life. Over time they were often dedicated to locally important or auspicious saints and honoured through annual celebrations. Well dressing is one of the most colourful and artistic of seasonal customs, comprising the decoration of wells and springs with flowers and other vegetative materials. Many villages still hold well dressing events across England, with a strong concentration in Derbyshire, where over eighty individual wells are dressed every year. They take place between Ascension Day (usually in May) through to early September, with many taking advantage of the floweriness of high summer, including July, for example, those in Buxton and Matlock. Some villages, such as Tissington, have several wells that are all decorated, creating an artistic trail for people to visit.

The basic principles of well dressing involve fixing nails to a flat wooden frame, which is then coated with a thick layer of mud or clay. Flower petals and other natural materials – such as leaves, moss and seed cones – are then pressed into the substrate to create a multi-coloured composite picture. Well dressing is a labour of love, needing plentiful patience and a high degree of manual dexterity, but the final results are widely admired and valued as an expression of local pride (as highlighted in the All's Well folk tale). Images range from Biblical scenes to topical events, and the parish church is often involved as a focal point for a dedication ceremony during the week of the well dressing. Many current customs are recent revivals, but contain echoes of much older traditions in venerating water sources. Wells were once a popular destination for spiritual pilgrimages, such as St Anne's in Bristol, which in recent years has reinvented a processional pageant around the well. The tradition of 'clootie wells' – tying pieces of coloured cloth to a thorn tree growing beside a well – has ancient pagan roots and is still observed in some locations, particularly in Scotland and Cornwall. Despite being later adopted as Christian sites, they maintain their aura of mystery and magic, and even an eerie atmosphere, reflecting tales of dark spirits lurking within the waters ...

Spirits of Place

The end of July, as school summer holidays begin, is the time when cautionary tales of dark dangers in the wild world perennially resurface. Certain wells and rivers, as well as trees and other natural features, are each guarded by its own *genius loci* – 'spirit of place'. The physical characteristics, and temperaments, of these site-specific sprites are often determined by the nature of their particular habitat. From widespread folklore, their function seems to be to either warn people away from natural hazards or to punish those who transgress natural laws; especially taking too soon or too greedily from nature's wild harvest.

One of the most infamous, and frightening, of these tutelary spirits is Jenny Greenteeth – the witch of the ditch. It is said her green, matted hair floats on the water as pondweed, while down below green, glowing eyes watch and green, bony fingers twitch – ready to snatch any child who strays too close to the water's edge! According to a local Lancashire legend, she was once a flesh-and-blood woman who, after being jilted at the altar, became bitter and twisted. At the peak of her misanthropic malevolence, she tried to pour poison down the village well, only succeeding in falling in and drowning herself. Since then, her malicious presence infuses stagnant waters and slow-flowing ditches – as Jenny Greenteeth.

Similar spiteful spirits are known from other watery places across northern parts of Britain. Peg Powler inhabits sluggish sections of waterways (especially the River Tees), Nelly Longarms lurking at the bottom of deep and murky ponds, while secluded marshes are infested by scaly creatures called Grindylows – small but supernaturally strong. In Scotland, the Shellycoat, as its name suggests, is covered in the shells of various water snails and rises up from streams to lead travellers astray. The Kelpie is a terrifying water horse that drags unsuspecting passers-by down to the bottom of Scottish rivers and freshwater lochs. In folk tales from the borders of England and Scotland, a creature called the Brown Man of the Moor holds sway in its deadly domain, marked by a bubbling brown burn.

Away from water, in the green woods of Yorkshire, Churn-milk Peg is a distinctive tutelary spirit who sits in the top branches of hazel trees, swirled in smoke from her long-stemmed pipe. Her name derives from the milky consistency of unripe hazelnuts in July (there's a male counterpart: a similarly named Melch Dick). Woe betide anyone Peg catches gathering hazelnuts out of season, for she's known to deliver a painful poke with her pipe, a sharp slap round the legs and strong words of rebuke:

Smoke! Smoke a wooden pipe!
Getting nuts before they're ripe!

Echoing such dangerous tales, the stillness of the air, the absence of birdsong and the stagnant waters can sometimes add an air of melancholy to the long days of July. However, staring into dark pools can also reveal deep insights. A well-known Celtic myth tells of an ancient hazel tree that once grew beside a well, with nine nuts that contained all the world's knowledge. Eventually, the nuts fell into the waters of the well, where they were eaten by a huge salmon. A powerful poet-druid of those times, seeking to absorb its wisdom, asked his apprentice to catch and cook the Salmon of Knowledge. The boy achieved his task, but burnt his thumb while roasting the fish on the fire and instinctively stuck it into his mouth to ease the pain. In doing so, all the knowledge drained from the fish and into the apprentice – who went on to become the legendary Irish hero Fionn mac Cumhaill.

Summer Saints

St Swithin's Day, if it does rain
Full forty days, it will remain.
St Swithin's Day, if it be fair
For forty days, t'will rain no more.

The latter part of July is famous for heavy, humid weather and summer showers. St Swithin's Day, on 15th July, marks one of the most well-known pieces of seasonal weather lore in Britain: if it rains on this date, then forty days of wet weather will follow; and vice versa if it's dry. Allegedly, the meteorological prophecy originated when the buried body of St Swithin (the Anglo-Saxon Bishop of Winchester) was moved from outside to inside the cathedral church, resulting in a supernatural rainstorm. The rain continued until his remains were eventually reinstated in their original resting place. Despite the high chance of thunderstorms and heavy rainfall at this time of year, thankfully the prediction of precipitation fails to live up to its full forty days these days. Nevertheless, July holds anxious times for farmers, who rely on a good spell of dry weather for harvesting hay and grain crops; as they literally look to the heavens for divine reassurance. By contrast, rain in the orchard was always welcomed on

St Swithin's Day, believed to be the saint himself christening the apple crop. Certainly, a healthy dose of rain helps the fruit to finish swelling before ripening over the following months. It is considered unseasonal to eat apples before this date: 'Til Swithin's Day be past, apples be not fit to taste.

There's a further procession of saints' days with watery connections through July. The 20th July is St Margaret's Day, the patron saint of shepherds, with heavy rainfall around this date once referred to as 'Margaret's floods'. The 25th July is the feast day of St James, the patron saint of fishermen, whose emblem is a scallop shell (still worn by pilgrims on the Camino Santiago in Spain). Traditionally this date marks the start of the oyster season and Whitstable Oyster Festival is still held on the nearest weekend to St James' Day, including a church blessing of its fisheries.

Flavour of the Month

Assam Tea, Meadowsweet and Foraged Fruits 'Mocktail'

While on a long, summer bicycle ride, it's worth keeping an eye out for wild raspberry plants in woodland edges at this time of year. Like the wild strawberry in June, it has much smaller fruit than cultivated varieties but packs a punch with fragrance and flavour – arguably the finest fruits on Earth and a precious prize if you manage to find any. Cherries, with their unique stone-fruit flavour, are best gathered with the hooked handled of a lace parasol. The parasol provides plentiful shade during refreshment stops as you cycle along. It's worth remembering where you spotted the mesmerising cherry blossom in the April–May spectacle, in order to re-find all its locations now. Some of these foraged fruits will be sour and tart; others will be adorably sweet and juicy.

Finally, if you breeze past any damp, soggy habitats, where the rushes grow, look out for the first unfurling flowers of meadowsweet. Living up to its name, it's another coumarin-rich plant, essentially 'free' vanilla in these isles, and an essential ingredient in this sour cocktail recipe; 'no and low' style. Assam tea gives a clever non-alcoholic nod to whisky and makes a very welcoming drink after a parched summer's afternoon on two wheels.

FOR THE AROMATIC BREW
    250ml Assam tea
    Half a handful of fresh meadowsweet flowers

– Brew a pot of Assam tea, infused with the fresh meadowsweet; makes enough for four servings.
– Strain after six minutes and allow to cool.

A SIMPLE SYRUP
    80g sugar
    80g water

Simple syrup is water and white sugar in equal parts, boiled then chilled. It will store refrigerated for a month.

TO SERVE (SHAKEN ONE AT A TIME)
    50ml Assam & meadowsweet tea
    25ml lemon juice strained of pulp
    ½ egg white
    20ml simple sugar syrup

– Add the ingredients to a cocktail shaker with plenty of ice.
– Agitate vigorously for twenty seconds, no less.
– Strain into a coupe glass, garnish with a foraged cherry and a wild raspberry.

Dog Days

The month of July takes its name from *Julius* Caesar, commemorating the death of the Roman dictator (it was originally pronounced like his name, as in 'Julie'). The term 'Dog Days' originated in Roman times, referring to a period of hot and sticky weather in July and early August. The Dog Star (Sirius) appears in the sky around sunrise at this time of year (specifically 3rd July to 11th August), and the Romans believed it added its own heat to that of the sun. Dog Days were considered a time of ill omen: when wine turned sour, dogs went mad and people suffered from all manner of malaises. According to folklore, this is also the time of year when demonic black dogs appear, with many local versions across Britain, including Old Shuck in Norfolk.

Moth Week and Flying Ant Day

The warmth of high summer, and the peak growth of grasses, give rise to a plethora of moths on the wing in July. The best way to appreciate the delight of these night-flying insects is by using a moth trap, making use of moths' innate attraction to artificial light. In the UK, the last full week of July is designated as National Moth Week, intended to inspire and encourage people to catch and record moths in their own local patch. If you haven't got a specially designed trap, it's possible to make your own simple version with just a torch and a white sheet. Despite a sharp decline in moth numbers in recent years (forty years ago 'moth snowstorms' were a common sight around street lights), their diversity in size, shape and pattern is still one of the wonders of the wild world. Their names are magical and evocative too: Hebrew Character, Beautiful Arches, True Lover's Knot and Elephant Hawk-moth; to name but a few. After a June dip, day-flying butterflies abound again this month, with handy, colour-coded species names, such as Meadow Browns, Holly Blues and Marbled Whites.

Sultry weather in July heralds another seasonal insect phenomenon: Flying Ant Day. This happens when winged individuals of several ant colonies emerge at the same time in one local area. July is also peak season for seeing glow-worms: their eerie pinpricks of yellowish-green light can be seen when walking along dark paths and unlit country lanes at night. More common than most people realise, their favoured habitats are uncut grassy verges and field edges. The abdomens of the flightless females emit a bioluminescent glow in order to attract the smaller males, which can sometimes be seen (by torchlight) clinging onto their backs. There are several, pleasingly unlikely, tales of glow-worms providing emergency illumination as bike lights, night-fishing floats and reading lamps.

The White Moth

Donald sat beside the flickering fire eating his supper alone, as he did every evening. Working as a fisherman on the west coast of Scotland, he was successful enough to lead a comfortable life, but he'd never found anyone to share it with him. That evening in late July, as the simmering sun was slowly sinking into the grey water of the loch, he heard a faint fluttering noise against the cottage window. Looking up, he saw a white moth dancing across the pane, occasionally dropping down to rest on the tall hollyhocks that grew against the cottage. Donald got up from his comfortable seat by the fire and opened the window. Immediately, the moth flew into the house and then up to the rafters of the roof, where it continued to flutter about excitedly. Unable to see clearly in the gathering gloom, Donald lit the rush lamp on the wall to shed a little light into the room. The moth slowly circled down, pulled inexorably towards the yellow light, until its delicate, dusty wings touched the flame. Suddenly there was a brilliant white flash and there, standing in front of him, was a young woman with a white dress and a bright smile.

'Who on earth are you?' stuttered Donald in astonishment.

'I was the moth at your window, dear Donald. And, if you'll have me, I've come to be your wife, so you need no longer sit on your own by the fire. My only condition is that you never again light a naked flame in the house, except for the fire in the hearth. If you do, I will be drawn towards it and you'll never see me again.'

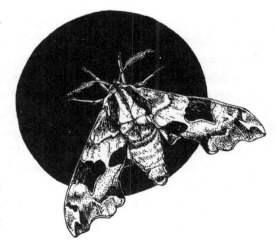

Without any hesitation, Donald agreed. The young woman proved to be an adorable, admirable companion and soon they were married in the local kirk, then settled down to a life of convivial contentment. Each evening, through the seasons, they sat by the window, or by the fireside, while the rush light remained unlit. However, the daughter of a neighbouring crofter had longed to marry Donald herself and was greatly aggrieved at this mysterious woman who'd suddenly arrived to be his bride. Brooding with bitterness, she often passed by the cottage in the evening to peer enviously through their window. Then one day, an opportunity presented itself: she overheard his new wife gently chiding Donald as he went to kindle the rush light. 'Careful, my love, remember that would be the end of me ...'

The following evening, while Donald was still out in his boat, the crofter's daughter knocked on the door of the house, pretending to be overcome with faintness. The fisherman's wife went outside to draw water, while the other woman quickly took a burning stick from the fire and lit the little rush light. As Donald's wife came back into the room, she dropped the cup of water and rushed towards the shimmering lamp – pulled by an irresistible force. As her body touched the flame, there was a flash of light and she disappeared. A white moth flew out of the open door and was taken away by the breeze. Donald, on his way home, saw the little moth flying feebly against the wind. In vain he ran after the fluttering creature in the darkness, towards the sea. Neither he, nor his moth wife, were ever seen again.

Fowl Play

The water theme is continued through July – in the shape of yellow rubber ducks! Annual duck racing events take place on watercourses across the UK, often timed for the start of the summer holidays. They often raise funds for charity by people sponsoring numbered ducks as they float down a netted section of the river, with prizes for the winners. This month's duck races include Ouseburn in Newcastle, Witham in Essex and Buxton (part of a two-week carnival with its own well dressing). Allegedly, duck racing began in Dyserth, in North Wales, although Grove in Oxfordshire once had a race with real live ducks, which disbanded in the 1960s.

'Swan upping' is the annual counting and marking of swans on the River Thames, and also in Abbotsbury, Dorset; which lays claim to being the only managed mute swan colony in the world. As a living tradition, with a noble heritage, swan upping remains a vibrant occasion at both these locations and also provides a valuable annual survey of the bird populations and their habitats.

Old Roots, New Shoots

THE WATERS OF LIFE

The warm, languid days of summer provide a wonderful opportunity to spend time in, on or beside water. Lazing around beside a lake or messing about on the river are timeless 'in-activities' – such moments of happy indolence being a net benefit to both the individual and the world as a whole. As many anglers know well, being quiet and still beside a watercourse allows rich opportunity for watching wildlife as it comes and goes, undisturbed by busyness.

Letting go of inclinations to dive for cover, summer downpours offer the sensual experience of being out in the rain; warm but soaked to the skin. Look out for eels, too, which are said to appear on land around rivers during thunderstorms.

For more vigorous types, wild swimming has become a popular activity in recent times, as a way of connecting with natural waterscapes, as well as revitalising our wild selves. Alternatively, take time to discover the source of a local river on foot, in a group perhaps, then marking and honouring the wellspring with some natural decoration and/or a spoken blessing. It might become an annual tradition, as with our 'well-dressed' ancestors. If a water source is hard to find, then try water divining with hazel.

Finally, the gentle meandering of summer streams and the reflective qualities of still water allow unhurried time for daydreaming; letting thoughts and ideas slowly bubble up to the surface. Such watery reveries have often been the stimulus, setting and subject for a flow of written words, such as those captured in *The River's Voice*, an anthology of poetry published by Common Ground as a celebration of our relationship with running waters.

8

August

When haying is over, then harvest draws near.
We will send to our brewer to brew us strong beer.
And in brewing strong beer, we will cut down their corn;
We will take it to the barn, boys, to keep it from harm.

The Strangers' Share

Before any of us, there was *them* – the Little People, the Good Neighbours, the Shining Ones, the Fair Folk, the Others, the Strangers. They've always been here, before us and then among us; right underneath our noses. But seldom seen, except by chance in the gleam of a stream or the flicker of firelight. But they can be heard, when they want to be, in the yelping of fox cubs or the plaintive cries of lapwings. And if you listen carefully, at the right time of day, you can hear their muffled music underneath the hills and their faint footsteps in the pitter-patter of raindrops.

The old folk heard them and knew they were there. They knew that on May Day Eve the Little People danced on round-crowned hills until daybreak, and that on Lammas Eve they gathered in the fields to feast and play their little fiddles, like crickets in the dusk. Those that worked the land – farmers, growers and shepherds – also knew that the Others were always in the thick of things in the fields: tweaking leaf buds in spring, wrestling with weeds in summer, ripening the ears of corn at harvest time. For a favoured few they would help with the work on the farm as well – threshing the wheat and filling the grain sacks overnight. Respectful of their existence, and grateful for their help, the old folk followed the Old Ways and kept the covenant of customs between us and them. They gave the Strangers a sheaf of wheat from the fields, or the first forkful of potatoes, or a cup of freshly picked berries, and they always made sure there was an apple left hanging on every tree in the orchard. They baked bread and cakes and left them out on flat stones by the riverside in the morning. And at night there was a corner of cheese and mug of harvest ale set beside the fireplace. Our ancestors did everything they possibly could to stay on good terms with the Good Neighbours.

But, somehow, in the slipping of time and the passing of generations, we began to overlook the Others; we became too busy to bother with superseded superstitions. Children grew into adults without ever hearing the stories of the Good Neighbours and, without stories to remind them, nobody remembered to leave them gifts of gratitude. Before long the Fair Folk were unfairly forgotten. But, even if we'd forgotten them, they hadn't forgotten us. In the end, they took ignorance as insolence – and fairies have always been easily offended by bad manners!

Suddenly, without the nurturing nature of the Others, the seedlings' growth in spring was stunted and weak, while pernicious weeds popped up everywhere. The grain harvests failed as blight and rust ravaged the crops, just as they were about to be gathered in. Thatches on houses collapsed, equipment broke down and every task that the farmworkers turned their hands to went 'arsy-versy'. With the rising anger of the Others, the weather itself became vicious and vindictive. Their icy bitterness became a frost that killed tender shoots and their tempestuous rage turned into storms that flooded the fields. Their vengeance rose like a tide of resentment as rain fell for days and days, downpour becoming deluge. Across the land, the living world that had once prospered with plenty, was now characterised by capricious cruelty: milk dried up in cows' udders, lambs were stillborn, ponies went lame, people became sick. Losing heart and hope, some abandoned working the land altogether. Until at last someone, one of the old folks that still remembered the Old Ways, uttered out loud the words that made sense of it all: 'The Others are against us! We've offended the Good Neighbours. We need to make our peace – restore the covenant of customs.'

Like rays of sunshine at dawn, the message crept quickly across the land – along highways and holloways, across fields and fens. The people knew what to do. They waited for the next new moon and then, in every corner of the countryside, they brought gifts of corn and cake, of bread and beer, and left them on flat rocks by the river and in the doorways of their empty barns. With caps in hands, the people addressed the unseen forces, 'Good Neighbours, here are gifts ... Hear our words of sorrow and remiss!'

They waited and listened. And for a long time, there was no reply — just the gentle lip-lapping of water and the whisper of the wind. But then the eerie cry of a barn owl, curdling the evening sky, followed by a soft singing sound from the hollow hills. Some people say they saw a flash of light on the stream, some heard a swishing in the grasses, others felt a cold kiss of little lips upon their cheeks. But after that, things did begin to get better. At last, the rain eased and the wind died down. Crops germinated and thrived in the fields, without being choked by weeds. The harvest was good, cattle chewed the cud, pigs put on weight and ewes gave birth to twins. The sick got better and soon children ran happy and healthy through the village streets. From then on, at every new moon — and also on Lammas Day — the people honoured the Strangers and left them their fair share of good fortune; keeping the covenant of customs.

A Mountain to Climb

In the Celtic calendar, 1st August is marked as Lughnasadh (pronounced loo-na-sa) — a seasonal celebration dedicated to a pagan god, named Lugh. He was famed as a leader of the legendary race of supernatural beings in Ireland known as the Tuatha de Danna, who, it's said, eventually became the Fair Folk. Lugh brought humanity the precious treasure of cereal grains, after defeating Balor, a dark god of the underworld. He is also credited with establishing the four agricultural seasons on Earth: spring sowing, summer ripening, autumn harvesting and winter feasting. As a bright god of the harvest, he was warmly celebrated by lighting hilltop bonfires on the Eve of August; a shared element with the other three Celtic fire festivals. Despite being seen as the last month of meteorological summer, in both farming and folklore such festivities at the beginning of August herald the onset of autumn.

The day itself was also observed by climbing a mountain or hill — to watch for incoming inclement weather that might affect the harvest and also to leave an offering for the fairies, hidden in their hollow hills. In Ireland, this tradition turned into Reek Sunday, which involves climbing Croagh Patrick — a summit named after the national Irish saint, who some see as a Christian version of the pagan Lugh. In appearance, Lugh was often represented as a fair-haired, youthful warrior and sometimes known as Lugh of the Long Hand, because of his skill with a spear. Lughnasadh is therefore also associated with athletics and physical games, still reflected in the Highland Games that take place in many different locations across northern Scotland during July and August.

This is also a traditional time of year to go foraging for wild berries, which ripen around the beginning of August. Small, purple bilberries – also known by other local names, such as whortleberries in the south-west and blaeberries in Scotland – provide sweet treats in the hills and highlands. Best eaten raw and on-the-go, they also make a tasty pie if you can be bothered to pick enough – they tend to be widely scattered. By contrast, bright scarlet berries of rowan (mountain ash) are easily gathered in bulk, then processed at home into jelly and wine.

First Fruits

At the Ould Lammas Fair boys were you ever there,
Were you ever at the Fair in Ballycastle-O?

Since Saxon times, 1st August has been know as *Hlaf-Maese*, meaning Loaf Mass, and commonly shortened to Lammas. It's a celebration of the beginning of the harvest – a festival of first fruits – and a cultural expression of gratitude for the successful completion of the farming cycle. The initial cut of the ripe cereal crop holds particular seasonal significance and is traditionally marked by baking a loaf of bread made from the first part of the harvest, decorated in the form of a wheat sheaf. Lammas loaves are still presented at the local churches on the nearest Sunday and lots of Lammas fairs are held annually across the UK. Importantly, this bread is to be shared with others in the community, including leaving a few crumbs in the four corners of the farmstead as the Strangers' Share; keeping the covenant of customs intact, as the story suggests. The importance and anticipation of the harvest led to the belief that no iron should be used on the land (i.e. harvesting should not begin) until Lammas Day itself. The Anglo-Saxon designation for a full moon in July is Grain Moon, or sometimes Barley Moon, acknowledging the importance of these essential cereal crops.

The term 'Lammas lands' denotes the return of common grazing lands after the cultivation of crops. 'Lammas growth' refers to a secondary flush of foliage on certain trees in early August, particularly oaks and ash, as an adaptation to leaf damage by insects. An alternative Anglo-Saxon name for the month of August was Woedmonath, literally meaning 'plant month', signifying the time of year for gathering and drying plants with special culinary or medicinal value.

Last Rites

Just as the first cut of the grain crop holds a sacred moment of communal gratitude, so too the last cut is steeped with seasonal significance. The spirit of the
corn is believed to reside in the final sheaf, and has various epithets in different
regions of Britain and Ireland: the neck, the mare, Old Sow, Cripple Goat. It
was unlucky for one person to be held responsible for killing the corn spirit,
so the last cut was traditionally undertaken by a group of harvesters throwing
their sickles at the same time. The act was accompanied by vocal ritual, called
'crying the neck', which is still enthusiastically enacted each year in several locations, most notably in Cornwall:

'I have it, I have it!'
'What have you got?'
'The neck, the neck!'

The severed 'neck' is then solemnly presented to the land in three different
directions (east, south and west, but not the north – the direction of winter
and bad weather). In past times, each team of harvesters was led by a designated
Lord of the Harvest. The last load of grain harvested from arable fields was
known as the Hockey Load and the wagon decorated with ribbons and flowers
as it was brought back for the last time in celebration.

Up! Up! Up! A happy harvest home!
We have sowed, we have mowed,
We have carried our last load!

After the main harvest was over, gleaners would be free to take their pickings
of the grain spilt on the ground. This often provided a vital seasonal commod-
ity for landless cottagers and poor parishioners, and was at one time enshrined
by law. In modern times, there has been a resurgence in the time-honoured
tradition of gleaning, making use of otherwise wasted food from a range of
agricultural crops. Leftover grains are also an important resource for seed-eating
birds and other wildlife on farmland. However, with more efficient farming
methods and widespread autumn sowing of crops, the window of opportunity
for wildlife to glean grains is much reduced. In folk tales, fairies are sometimes
portrayed as gleaners, gathering what we don't need ourselves, while keeping the farm in good order. As ever, it's always prudent to make sure we leave
enough supplies for the Good Neighbours.

Corn Dollies

The last sheaf of the harvest is also traditionally used to make a 'corn dolly' – a human figure or abstract design twisted into shape from the residual straw. Traditional (longer-stemmed) varieties of cereals produce the best dollies, and there's still plenty of passion and creativity that goes into their design and craft, drawing on both local styles and personal preferences. Usually, they are given feminine form, varying from corn babies to corn maidens or even old crones. In origin, these may represent Mother Nature as a general symbol for feminine fertility and productivity. Alternatively, they may reflect pre-Christian deities associated with the harvest; notably Ceres, the Roman goddess of agriculture and cereal crops, and Demeter, her counterpart from ancient Greece. In any case, the carefully crafted straw figures are believed to hold the embodied spirit of the corn safe until the following growing season, when they are ploughed back into the earth to restart the seasonal cycle (see January). It's worth noting that the Old English word 'corn', related to kernel, refers to all types of cereal grains; whereas its modern use often specifies maize, i.e. sweetcorn.

As an ongoing tradition, corn dollies provide both a practical approach and meaningful imagery for savouring the season and reconnecting with the land, when far fewer of us work directly on it. Scarecrow festivals have had something of a revival in recent years, with many local annual events now held across the UK during August. These much larger straw-filled human effigies reflect both the traditions and materials of harvest time, as well as portraying modern themes.

A Grain of Truth – Cut and Come Again

A recurring theme behind many harvest rituals is death and resurrection: the Corn Spirit, or Earth Mother, sacrifices life in order to give life to us. The annual Burning of the Bartle folk custom in North Yorkshire, held on St Bartholomew's Day (24th August), also echoes such seasonal sentiments. A larger-than-life figure, also made from recently cut straw, is paraded through the village of West Witton before being ceremonially burnt, with plenty of ale-fuelled enthusiasm. There are various theories as to the origins of Bartle – from prehistoric giant to St Bartholomew himself – but it certainly seems to invoke the principle of an annual sacrifice to renew the cycle of life. The Celtic harvest god Lugh, described above, also gained ascendency through death: killing and taking the place of a rival deity in order to bring us life-giving cereals. However, the most striking personification of the sacrificial harvest in British folklore is John Barleycorn; whose mythical narrative holds the life cycle of sown seed to harvest ale. He can also be seen, perhaps, as an autumnal incarnation of May's Green Man; green foliage now replaced by golden sheaves of corn. His tale is lyrically, and graphically, told through the lyrics of this well-known traditional ballad:

John Barleycorn

There were three men, came to the west, their fortunes for to try,
And these three men made a solemn vow: John Barleycorn should die.
They ploughed, they sowed, they harrowed him in, threw clods all on his head.
And these three men made a solemn vow: John Barleycorn was dead.
They let him lie for a very long time, till rain from heaven did fall,
Then little Sir John sprung up his head and so amazed them all.
There he stood in summer's sun, till he was both pale and wan,
And little Sir John's grown a long, long beard and so became a man.
Then they hired men with the scythes so sharp to cut him off at the knee,
They rolled him and tied him 'round the waist and served him barbarously:
Then more men came with crab-tree sticks to cut him; skin from bone,
The miller treated him worse than that and ground him between two stones.
Here's little Sir John and in the nut-brown bowl and brandy in the glass
And little Sir John and in the nut-brown bowl proved the strongest man at last.
For the huntsman he can't hunt the fox, nor loudly blow his horn
And the tinker, he can't mend his pots without John Barleycorn.

Beer Necessities

Oh good ale, you are my darling,
You are my joy both night and morning!

Good ale is both subject matter and lubrication for singing folk songs, such as 'John Barleycorn', at this time of year. Another well-known traditional song, called 'The Barley Mow', requires participants to tip their tankards regularly during its recitation, as directed by the lyrics themselves. Beer – the liquid equivalent of bread, perhaps – is an essential ingredient of harvest celebrations, providing both the reason and the rhyme for the merrymaking. Whereas, 'small beer' (lower in alcohol) was often for labourers working in the corn fields, strong ale was expected as reward at the end of the harvest. The onus was on the Lord of the Manor to provide sufficient quantity and quality of ale to satisfy thirsty throats and festive spirits. Britain has long enjoyed a pre-eminent reputation in the making and drinking of beer, with both brewers and landlords esteemed on the quality (and quantity) of their ale.

Golden Ale

There once was a farmer called Willie, who lived with his old mother in west Wales. When not working on the farm, he loved to make home-brewed beer to share with his farming friends. Unfortunately, no matter how much he experimented with the proportions of malt, yeast and hops, the resulting ale was always weak and watery – and much-derided by those who tasted it. One morning, Willie's mother was sweeping the threshing floor at harvest time, when she heard a thin, small voice coming from a dark corner of the room, politely asking to borrow a sieve. Being someone who followed the Old Ways, she recognised this must be one of the Tylwyth Teg – the Fair Folk. So straight away she found a sieve from Willie's brewing shed and placed it carefully in the corner of the threshing room. A few days later Willie was making another batch of beer, when he noticed a feint, golden glow on the same sieve. Unbeknownst to him, the fairies had used it to sift the dust from their hoard of gold and left a layer of shimmering magic behind. By the end of the month, he turned the tap on the barrel of beer and was astonished by the freshness and flavour of the frothing golden ale that came pouring out. That evening, at a drinking session in the barn, his friends agreed: it was the finest ale any of them had ever tasted; and very pleasing in its intoxicating after-effects, too. Before long both Willie's beer and his company were in great demand. For a happy, hazy year he revelled in his new-found fame and fortune as a brewer of 'golden ale'.

The following August, however, while Willie was boasting to his mother about his brewing skill over a lunch of bread and beer, she suddenly remembered that the Tylwyth Teg had borrowed his old sieve. 'They must have left a trace of their fairy magic on it, that's why your ale tastes so good!' Well, no sooner spoken than broken. Fairy gifts should never be talked about openly and fairy gold can quickly turn to dust. Sure enough, the next batch of beer he brewed was completely lacking in both its golden lustre and fine flavour. His reputation sank as swiftly as it had risen. Nevertheless, Willie continued to revel in the fact that he'd once brewed the best ales in Wales.

Hops and Heather

Hops, one of the distinctive flavourings of ale, are usually harvested in late August and early September. Different varieties of English hops have colourful names, such as Goldings, Fuggle and Boadicea. Many pubs still hang bines of hops above the bar, with new season's flowers brought in by the front door as the old ones are taken out by the back, to ensure the landlord's good fortune. In the recent past, the hop harvest was carried out by whole communities travelling from cities to rural farms, notably London to Kent. Hop Hoodening festivals merrily marked the end of the harvesting period, with a hop king and queen leading the celebrations. One or two still take place in some places where hops are grown, including Faversham and Canterbury. Smaller wild-growing

hops can also be found in flower among hedgerows in August; adding their own locally distinctive flavours to home brews. At Cerne Abbas brewery in Dorset, they collaboratively brew a 'community hop' beer each year using hop flowers foraged by local people – contributors receive plenty of good ale in exchange.

August is also the month when the flowering of heather bushes reaches a peak of perfection – with whole hillsides covered in a purple haze in the northern uplands of Britain. Before hops, heather was traditionally used as flavouring in beer, with ancient pedigree in Scotland especially. One local legend tells of a Pictish chieftain captured by the Vikings who refused to reveal his tribe's recipe for heather ale. In the end, his family were murdered on the hillside – the heather flowers turning purple from the shedding of royal blood. According to another Scottish tale, rare white heather flowers originated from the tears of a highland princess, whose lover was killed in battle on the eve of their wedding. Patches of white-flowering heather are also said to indicate where fairies bury their dead.

A Good Crop of Fairy Tales

The 1st May to 1st August marks the span of the lightest, brightest quarter of the year and the main period of growth for most crops in northern Europe. It is correspondingly fertile with folklore. In particular, the opening and closing of this period, Beltane and Lammas, are highly charged with magic and mystery; a ripe time for otherworldly goings-on. British and Irish folk tales offer plentiful examples of the Little People helping with the work of harvest time and other anonymous acts of spontaneous generosity. However, many tales also reveal the Others as being both easily offended and prone to considerable capriciousness. As well as a lack of gratitude, notably neglecting to leave them seasonal gifts, they dislike close scrutiny or interference in their seelie affairs. One such story tells of a farmer in Scotland, with more lands than hands, whose grain harvest was cut and threshed each year by invisible helpers. Grateful for their assistance, a portion of bread and mug of beer were duly left in the barn at dusk. However, one night he made the rash decision of staying awake in order to count how many of the fairy folk were helping him. The Good Neighbours disappeared as soon as they discovered his prying eyes and he never received their assistance again.

Neither are the Little People backwards at *taking* whatever they want, with harvest time often the seasonal setting for dark tales of human abductions. In particular, there are many 'changeling' stories of human babies being myste-riously swapped for fairy replacements – equally tiny, wrinkly and toothless beings, but altogether less innocent! In one such tale, a woman suspects her twin children are changelings and pretends to brew ale for the farmworkers in an eggshell over the fire, at which point they start to chuckle to each other, before one speaks out loud:

Acorn before oak I knew,
And an egg before a hen,
But never I heard of an eggshell
Brew a drink for harvest men.

The Fair Folk are also said to hold their own seasonal celebrations at this numi-nous time of year. A haunting folk tale recounts how a young farmer, on his way to a local harvest festival, inadvertently stumbles across a fairy feast at Selena Moor, in Cornwall. While there he sees a former sweetheart, who'd been missing for months and presumed dead. In fact, she'd been taken by the fairies to bake bread and brew beer for them, as well as look after the human children among them. Intending to rescue her, he turned his coat inside out and threw it into the fairy throng – only for the whole gathering to disappear in the blink of an eye. He never saw his sweetheart again.

Fossilised sea urchins are colloquially known as 'fairy loaves', perhaps due to their similarity in appearance to small bread rolls. It used to be considered good fortune to keep them near the place where loaves were baked, either as an offering to the Fair Folk or to ward away their malevolent intent. According to one folklore tradition, a household that had a fairy loaf would never lack bread to eat.

A Plum Job

He who plants plums, plants for his sons.
He who plants damsons, plants for his grandsons.

August is the very beginning of the orchard fruit harvest, which slowly ripens over the next few months. It begins with plums, in all their various colours and flavours, with National Plum Day held in August each year, and an annual festival in Pershore, Worcestershire.

One sunny afternoon in August, two young brothers were picking plums from a productive old tree in their grandmother's garden. The little, glistening globes were swollen with summer sweetness and the boys crammed as many into their own mouths as they placed in the wicker basket that they'd been given to fill. After some time, one of them wiped his juice-streaked lips and suddenly said, 'Brother, do plums have legs?'

'Don't be daft, of course not!' came the incredulous reply.

'Oh dear, I think I've just eaten a big spider then!'

Pickled Green Stone Fruits

Numerous cultivars of plums, apricots and damsons await our picking in August. Our walls are full of them, espaliered to take advantage of the warm, sheltered bricks. When eaten against custard and a sweet, brittle-baked crumble topping, the damson's sharp, tart fruit is particularly recommended.

However, hungry birds and wasps lie in wait if we can't get to them fast enough as they mature. So, to get ahead of the sun's ripening arc, we use a fascinating technique to preserve any thinned, under-ripe stone fruit: salt pickling. This creates an excellent larder ingredient that keeps for many months ahead, which is nutritious and pro-biotic. The sharp tang of green pickled plums heightens many dishes – certainly grilled meats and most picnic fare; but feel free to experiment.

    Under-ripe damsons or plums
    30g sea salt per kilo of jar space
    Fresh dill or fennel fronds
    Star anise
    Black cardamom pods
    Cherry (or oak) leaves
    Suitably sized preserving jars with lids
    Water, boiled and cooled

– Gather whole unripe plums or damsons straight into preserving jars, to fill as many as you want. To get to the correct pickling ratio, we have listed the salt per kilo of jar space. In this method, the whole fruit will take up approximately two-thirds of a jar's space, the rest taken up by water. When the salt permeates through the entire volume of fruit, it will end up at 3 per-cent of volume. In a jar of 500g total volume, you'll only need 15g of salt.
– Pre-heat an oven to 130°C.
– Rinse the stone fruit.
– Wash your glass jars and lids, add to a baking tray and place in the oven for eight minutes to sterilise. Allow jars to cool.
– Add a couple of tannic-rich cherry, or oak leaves. Add the stone fruit followed by salt and spices of choice, two or three of each, followed by the cooled kettle water to cover the fruit.
– Lid securely and stand at room temperature for five days in a baking tray, which will catch any leakage. The stone fruit will change colour as the fruit sours. Open only after five days to taste and store refrigerated from there on.

The plumpest and grandest patches of blaeberries can be discovered while bouncing over spring-coiled heather hills. The most challenging part to gathering wild bilberry is getting them home un-squished but freeze your pickings even part-pulped; they'll be a welcome addition to the hedgerow ketchup recipe in November.

Revelling in the Occasion

Dry August and warm, does the harvest no harm.

The cereal harvest needs to be brought in quickly to avoid wet weather and before the grains deteriorate. In the past, whole communities were involved in the work of the harvest, including women and children – with the school summer holidays arranged around this demanding agricultural period. Once safely gathered in, the celebrations were just as important. Many towns and villages in Britain held their own Wakes Weeks – a communal annual holiday, often timed according to the feast day of the local church's dedicated saint. The word originally stems from staying awake during a church vigil on holy days and is similarly used in funeral wakes, where mourners would stay up to keep the departing soul company. Religious piety, however, was soon subverted as a much-needed opportunity for social gatherings, especially for remote rural workers and seasonally employed travelling folk. Over time the festivities shifted from specific saints' days towards one convenient focal point in the year – after the harvest in late August. As ever, eating and drinking were important elements, often with regionally specific foodstuffs coming to the fore. The brewing of 'church ales' provided a steady flow of beer to quench revellers' thirsts and simultaneously raise funds for church-administered charities.

Many annual sheep fairs and horse fairs traditionally took place at this time of year; happily mixing agricultural trading with communal merrymaking. A few still survive, although much changed, such as Appleby Horse Fair in Cumbria. The legacy of post-harvest partying is sustained in having a bank holiday at the end of August (in England and Wales) and various modern-day festive events, including Notting Hill Carnival.

Old Roots, New Shoots

THE STAFF OF LIFE

Loaf Mass is a lesser-known celebration nowadays, perhaps, yet offers ongoing resonance for savouring the season. With Mother Nature's arms wide open, August is a good time for cultivating cultural gratitude. One practical way to acknowledge and share the abundance of the harvest is by baking bread – 'the staff of life' – to share with friends and neighbours (as well as strangers). Giving away home-baked (or home-brewed) gifts as an act of unprompted generosity can ripple out in neighbourhoods and local communities, like a cascade of kindness. The word companion, from its French roots, means 'with bread' – as in the person you share bread with on a journey. It's a timely reminder to take a wild walk with choice companions, to raise a hilltop toast to bright Lugh, then share a bread-based picnic, perhaps finishing with freshly picked bilberries. Gardens and allotments also offer rich pickings in August, with many vegetable varieties cropping heavily – notably, freshly dug potatoes (another harvest staple) providing a celebratory taste of the earth. Redistributing such 'growing wealth' is often as valued by the donors as much as the recipients; finding a good home for the glut! The corn crops and nature's first fruits are happily harvested in August: but its traditions and stories remind us not to forget the Strangers' Share. Breaking bread, sharing with serendipitous strangers as well as friends, offers a chance to restore the covenant of customs – honouring the Others, as we ask for blessings on the next cycle of crops.

> Good luck to the hoof and horn,
> Good luck to the flock and the fleece,
> Good luck to the growers of corn,
> With blessings of plenty and peace.

9

September

Autumn comes, but let us be glad
Singing an autumn tune,
Hearts will be lighter, nights be brighter,
Under the Harvest Moon.

The White Hare

Not so long ago, many country folk supplemented their meagre incomes from agricultural labour by foraging for food in the wild. In those days, in a small Dorset village nestled among low-lying hills, there were four farmworkers who often hunted together in the evenings. They couldn't afford guns, but each man had his own 'longdog' – an old Dorset breed well-suited to running over rough terrain – to help them catch wild game. They hunted whatever fare was there for the taking: pheasants, deer, rabbits and hares; always seasonal, but not necessarily legal. In the ancient alliance between humankind and canine, more often than not there was something for the pot.

On the days when the men went hunting after work, they were in the habit of leaving their tools at the cottage of an old woman who lived by herself, just beyond the village. There were some villagers, suspicious and small-minded folk, who called the old woman a witch and blamed her for all manner of malaises and mishaps. Yet there were others who secretly beat a path to her door by moonlight – seeking her help. To all who came, she listened deeply, before dispensing herbal remedies or healing words. The hunters themselves rarely saw the woman, as she was often away from the cottage at dawn and dusk. But they often left her a little loaf of barley bread on her doorstep, by way of thanks.

One evening in early September, just after the last of the crops had been safely gathered in, the four men set out hunting – hoping for a meaty treat to grace their harvest suppers. Not far from the old woman's cottage, they suddenly caught a glimpse of something mysterious: a pure white hare. They watched as it raced over a stubble field before darting down the river valley, and disappeared into a dense copse of trees. From then on, they talked more and more about catching this rare and magical creature. But try as they might they never got close – the hare proved too cunning for the hunters and too fast for their dogs. Like many men then, however, they were proud and stubborn; keen to prove their prowess as hunters. Over the following few days they laid their plans, waiting for the right moment to put them into action.

It came on a soft autumn evening, with the Harvest Moon rising huge and heavy above the ridgeway, as they spotted the white hare once more, nimbling along the edge of the copse. Some of the men sent their dogs running along the treeline to flush the hare out into the open. When the startled hare saw them, she ran like white lightning, zig-zagging across the field – her ears flat against her body, her back legs stretching beyond the front legs as she raced forward, quickening her pace all the time. She soon outdistanced the chasing longdogs. However, with the hounds still in pursuit, she was forced towards the only way out of the field: a gateway between a thick hedge of hawthorn and holly. And there, hiding on the other side, were two more men with two more dogs. As the hare ran through the gateway, the dogs were released from their leashes ...

Suddenly, the still evening air was pierced by the sound of frenzied snarling and then a high-pitched squeal. The dogs ripped and wrenched, they bit and broke, until eventually the hare was tossed into the air like a rag doll; white fur now flecked with red blood. It landed – not back on the ground, nor in the jaws of the dogs – but on top of the thorny hedge. Although badly wounded, the hare summoned the last of her strength to scramble, painfully, along the top of the hedge into the safety of the wild woods.

Hunters and dogs searched and sniffed for an hour or more, without sight or scent of the hare. Finally, they admitted defeat. The dogs were clipped onto their tethers and the men made their way back to the old woman's cottage to retrieve their tools. When they arrived, the door was ajar. And as they peered inside the cottage, their faces drained of colour. There, lying on the floor in a mangled heap, with torn clothes and bleeding body, was the old woman. Filled with a mixture of fear and guilt, the men quickly grabbed their tools and ran from the cottage. All except one – the youngest of the four hunters. He realised

the old woman was still breathing so lifted her body, as light as a bird, onto the bed. All night long he stayed by her bedside, tending the fire and holding her head as he gave her tiny sips of water from a cup. Eventually, in the pale morning light, she opened her bruised eyes and was able to speak. She told the young man how to make an infusion from dried herbs in jars on the shelves around the room. Following her instructions, he made the medicinal brew, then went to fetch fresh food from the village. He stayed in the cottage for two weeks, nursing the old woman until she'd regained her strength and her wounds were almost healed. Then, one morning, she held his hand and looked at him with a wrinkled smile, releasing him from his duties.

After that, the men never saw the white hare; not that they ever thought of hunting her again. However, some Dorset folk, when out walking by the light of a Harvest Moon, claim to have caught sight of a flash of white fur, streaking across the green fields.

Fair Game

The 1st September is the feast day of St Giles, who increased in both popularity and associated legends during the Middle Ages. He was also known as Giles the Hermit and was said to have travelled the countryside with a pet deer, which he protected religiously. Eventually he was killed by a hunter's arrow, as he protected the deer. St Giles Fairs were once a major seasonal event, continuing the 'wakes' traditions of August into early September. Oxford still holds one of the biggest St Giles Fairs, which takes place on the first Monday and Tuesday of September. The first day of September is also known colloquially as St Partridge Day, as it's the start of the hunting season for these game birds, as well some types of wildfowl.

The hare, first encountered in the springing folklore of March, leaps back into view in September; at the opposite side of the calendar clock. These shape-shifting white hares seem to embody the subtle moments of change at the two equinoxes, carrying the seasons on their fleet feet. This time, rather than bringing the dawning light of spring, a mysterious white hare leads us from autumn's harvest fields towards the dark woods of winter. Hares are widely associated with the moon, as elusive and enigmatic as its silvery light, and in imagery are often portrayed staring skywards: moon-gazing. It was once believed that hares could change gender during every full moon. They are still a magical sight to behold by moonlight on a mild autumnal evening. Although hares have a long history of being hunted and eaten as a game animal, there's plenty of superstition surrounding them. A famous Middle English poem, called 'The Names of the Hare', vividly strings together a long list of epithet for the hare that should be ritually recited before attempting to hunt one:

> To speak the praises of the hare,
> Then the man will better fare.
> His name is hedge-springer, dew-hopper,
> Stubble-stag and herb-cropper.
> The creep-along, the sitter-still,
> The pintail, the ring-the-hill ...

Shine On, Harvest Moon

In contrast to the flowery names of summer months, September rather prosaically takes its Latin designation from simply being the seventh month in the Roman calendar year (which commenced in March). However, the evocatively named Harvest Moon usually falls during September – the most well-known of all the Anglo-Saxon full moons through the lunar cycle of the year. As with calculating the date of Easter, September is the time when lunar and solar calendars are annually realigned; setting the rest of the year's seasonal celebrations in tune. The Harvest Moon is determined as the full moon closest to the date of the autumn equinox (usually falling on either 22nd or 23rd September), with all the subsequent named moons following in order. The term Harvest Moon was originally used to celebrate the time when the grain harvest was safely gathered in. Similarly, one of the Anglo-Saxon names for the month September was Haligomonath – meaning 'holy month' because of the religious ceremonies associated with the end of the harvest. Modern-day harvest festivals are relatively recent in origin, started by a parish priest in Cornwall in the 1840s, with displays of autumnal crops and produce, which are still widely held in churches and schools across the UK.

In earlier times, cereal crops were largely harvested in August as they ripened, but as fields and farms increased in size over the years, the harvest period necessarily extended into September. For a few successive nights the Harvest Moon rises soon after sunset, providing almost continual light for fieldworkers to carry on working into the night to bring in the last of the harvest. Despite popular belief, however, a Harvest Moon isn't bigger or brighter than other full moons, but appears more prominent as it stays close to the horizon for longer, often with a conspicuous reddish-orange glow. As well as featuring heavily in British folklore and folk songs, the Harvest Moon also plays a prominent seasonal role in East Asian culture and folk tales. The date of the Harvest Moon is celebrated as an annual Mooncake Festival, with lunar lanterns and special cakes left out to honour a Chinese goddess who was immortalised by becoming part of the moon.

In modern paganism, the celebration of the autumn equinox is sometimes referred to as Mabon, after the deity Mabon ap Modron from Welsh mythology, whose name translates as 'great son'. On the whole, however, the seasonal resonance of the Harvest Moon, as well as the well-kept traditions of Michaelmas (see below), have tended to eclipse the equinox as a celebration of mid-autumn.

Going Underground

The vernal and autumnal equinoxes, in March and September, hold the tipping points of the year, between light and dark. Between them they also frame the beginning and end of the story of Persephone, a well-known ancient Greek myth that tells the origins of the seasons. Persephone was the beloved daughter of Demeter – the Greek goddess of growth, agriculture and the harvest. Because of the infatuation of Hades, the god of the underworld, Persephone is fated to spend half the year in the dark realm of the dead, from the autumn equinox onwards. There, as the queen of the underworld, she guides lost souls across the River Styx, as they arrive after death. During this time, the emotions of her mother, Demeter, correspondingly plunge into the depths of despair: the light fades, the vegetation dies, the world withers down into winter.

Legging It

As Demeter's seasonal sorrow seeps across the natural world, September often brings a mini-stampede of little legs. Craneflies (also known as daddy long legs) and harvestmen (so called as they appear after the harvest) are suddenly everywhere – gardens are covered with spiders' webs, glistening with dew, and verges are ringing with the sound of crickets singing. Also, if you listen carefully, there's high-pitched squeaking among the long grasses, as shrews, mice and voles reach their peak populations – happy hunting for barn owls and kestrels, foxes and weasels …

Heron, Weasel and Bramble

Once upon a time, Heron, Weasel and Bramble all lived and worked together on a small farm. Between the three of them, somehow, the first year went well. So, after selling the produce they shared out the money and went their separate ways. Heron, being a careful creature, put her coins in a leather purse strung around her long neck, as she flew along the river. Admiring her own reflection, however, she bent her head downwards and the purse slipped down into the water. Ever since then, Heron has been stalking the river, on her long legs, searching for the lost purse. Wily Weasel bought a bag of grain, planning to sow another field of cereals – and make more money. While looking for land, however, a mischief of mice and rats nibbled a hole in the sack, stealing all the grains. Since then, in revenge, Weasel has ferociously hunted for small rodents. Lastly, Bramble blithely lent her cash to a passing traveller, who promised profusely to bring it back. But he never returned, and the money was never repaid. And ever since, prickly Bramble has snagged the clothes of every person who passes by, thinking it might be the one who stole her money long ago.

A Hedgerow Harvest

What's green as grass but grass it's not,
Then white as snow but snow it's not,
Then red as blood but blood it's not,
And black as coal but coal it's not?

The Anglo-Saxon name for a full moon in late August or early September, preceding the Harvest Moon, is Fruit Moon. It heralds a time when plums, pears and the first dessert apples are harvested in the orchard. In the wild, a rummage along any uncut hedgerow at this time of year offers a ripe harvest of nature's sweet treats. Scrambling brambles abound with succulent blackberries, ready to stain fingers and tongues. As the season proceeds, they mature from the tip of

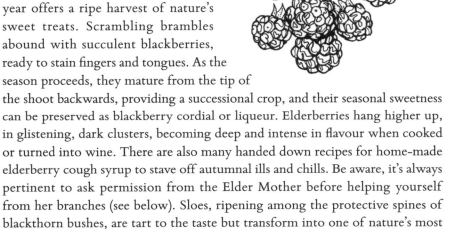

the shoot backwards, providing a successional crop, and their seasonal sweetness can be preserved as blackberry cordial or liqueur. Elderberries hang higher up, in glistening, dark clusters, becoming deep and intense in flavour when cooked or turned into wine. There are also many handed down recipes for home-made elderberry cough syrup to stave off autumnal ills and chills. Be aware, it's always pertinent to ask permission from the Elder Mother before helping yourself from her branches (see below). Sloes, ripening among the protective spines of blackthorn bushes, are tart to the taste but transform into one of nature's most delightful and delicious tipsy tipples: sloe gin. For connoisseurs of home-made booze, blackberry syrup, elderberry wine and sloe gin can be combined to make an exquisite and earthy 'hedgerow port'.

Autumnal yields of hazelnuts have nourished humans since the first hunter-gatherers, although as soon as they start to turn from green to pale gold there's competition from a ruthless rush of furry nibblers. In some regions of England, children were once given a day off school in September in order to go nutting! Once safely gathered, however, the nuts can be squirreled away for later leisurely consumption; roasted on the fire as the wild weather blows outside. The Anglo-Saxon word *haesel* translates as hat or bonnet, referring to the frilly fringe neatly fitted around the hard husks. Crab apples also abound in early autumn hedgerows, although, as their name suggests, they are generally sour and unpleasant, even when ripe – giving rise to the word 'crabby'. They were once widely used in fermented form as 'verjuice', an indigenous version of lemon juice, and they can also be roasted as a sweet-sour accompaniment for cooked meat.

September blow soft,
Till the fruit's in the loft.

Before the much-loved apple has its day in October, September is a time to savour and celebrate the humble but home-grown pear as they come into season in orchards and gardens. Look out for Wardens, a traditional variety of small, dark-coloured pear, thought to have originated from Warden Abbey in Bedfordshire. Warden pies, a sweet dish made from these pears flavoured with spices, are baked at this time of year; once served at Bedford Michaelmas Fair.

The Flying Pear Tree

Once, in old Gloucestershire, there was an old pear tree, growing on an old farm. The farmer loved the tree and its golden fruits, which hung heavy on the branches in September. But he hated the rooks that came every year to perch in the branches and peck at the pears. Eventually he'd had enough. One autumn morning, bright and early, he came out of the farmhouse with a loaded shotgun to shoot some of the thieving birds; hoping to deter the rest for good. But rooks, like all members of the crow family, are cunning creatures – they quickly flew away before he got close. The farmer, however, was determined to get the better of the black-feathered fiends. The following day he bought a pot of birdlime and painstakingly painted it on all the branches of the pear tree. Sure enough, the next time the parliament of rooks took their seats, their scaly feet were glued tightly to the tree. Now the farmer could take his time in taking his aim ...

But he must have been a terrible shot, because the gun fired – twice – harmlessly over the top of the tree. The stuck rooks were instantly startled into a riotous commotion, flapping their wings furiously. Before the farmer could load his shotgun again, a strange sucking sound filled the air as the roots of the tree were pulled out of the soft ground. The flying tree began to soar across the sky, travelling north for several miles, until eventually crossing the border into Herefordshire. There it began to rain, dissolving the glue and releasing the rooks' claws as they finally flew free from the branches. The tree plummeted heavily down to the ground, where it sunk into the rain-sodden soil. It soon re-rooted, growing well in its new setting for many more years – producing a good crop of golden pears every September – free for all.

Nasturtium & Pear Tonic

Amid the rush to gather and preserve the seemingly endless supply of autumn fruits and vegetables in the prolific walled garden, we often turn our attention to a valuable creeping plant, nasturtium. Never forget that this self-seeding plant, entirely edible from root to flower, might slip quietly away into winter soon – a shame to miss her delectable flavours. Gathering the seeds for sowing elsewhere, we also harvest the green parts before they die back and reach for a pioneering method of preservation that utilises the deep cold of your freezer to capture the charm of her last offering.

When trying to capture the essence of herbs in alcohol spirits (vodka or gin), it's disappointing to find that the fresh plants degrade to an underwhelming lawnmower clipping scent after a few days at room temperature. However, if you bring the deep frost of the freezer into the equation, we can preserve and capture all the vitality and freshness.

700ml Black Cow vodka stored in the freezer (brilliantly made from the discarded whey of UK milk)
Ten stalks and leaves of nasturtium
A pinch of sea salt

– Wash and tenderly dry the nasturtium leaves, checking the undersides for the tiny black aphids that gardeners appreciate the plant for as it attracts them away from their more beloved crops.
– Remove a little vodka from the bottle, take a sip, then blame it on 'the Angel's share'!
– Add the green plant to the spirit with a pinch of sea salt. Cap and shake the bottle, returning it to the freezer for two days before consumption. The vodka will then be imbued with all the fresh, spicy and redolent fragrances.
– Keep the nasturtium vodka frozen at all times, opening only to mix.

350ml or 12oz glass
35ml frozen nasturtium vodka
35ml pear juice
150ml tonic
130g ice
One fresh pear, sliced.
Garnish with a blackberry and pear slices

– Add the ingredients to a heavy-bottomed whisky glass, add the ice and stir a few times before serving.

This drink will take you back to the day you harvested this astonishing little garden plant.

Michaelmas

One Michaelmas morning I woke in a fright,
So I went to get up before it was light.
The morning being fine I thought I would roam,
So I took myself down by a blackberry grove.

The 29th September marks the feast day of St Michael, the only Christian saint who is also an archangel: famous for defeating Lucifer, the fallen angel. Michaelmas is correspondingly given much prominence within the seasonal calendar, celebrated at a crucial turning point of the year for farming and in the cultural calendar. Michaelmas Day is also one of the four 'quarter days' in England – a time for hiring fairs when workers would seek new employments and lodgings.

Eat a goose on Michaelmas Day,
Want not for money nor debts to pay.

Geese were traditionally roasted and eaten for Michaelmas festivities, after a final fattening up on spilt grains among stubble fields at this time of year. The droving of large gaggles of geese, on foot, from rural areas to towns and cities, led to several famous goose fairs, such as Tavistock in Devon and Nottingham. The latter still takes place, usually in early October now. Egremont Crab Fair in Cumbria, one of the longest-running fairs in England, is still held around Michaelmas. Nothing to do with crustaceans, it's named after crab apples that are given away during a Parade of the Apple Cart. The fair is also world-famous for its 'gurning' competition – pulling a funny face while framed by a horse harness, with the twisted expressions of participants said to be a reflection of the sourness of crab apples!

In Ireland, Michaelmas pie is a celebratory, seasonal dish that makes good use of the blackberries and apples available in hedges and orchards. In Scotland, an enriched bread called St Michael's bannock (see October's recipe), is baked by farming households on Michaelmas Eve. Traditionally, it contains barley, oats and rye in the particular proportions of the grains as they were harvested from the farm. One corner of the bannock should also be broken off and burnt in the hearth, before being thrown over the shoulder to ward away the Devil – St Michael's ancient adversary, who also looms large at this time of year.

The Devil of a Time

Late September, as the days are noticeably darkening, is the time when Old Nick makes his own infernal mark on the seasonal calendar. According to widely observed folklore, the Devil spits (some say urinates) over unpicked blackberries on Michaelmas Day, rendering them unfit for human consumption after then. According to legend, when the Devil was expelled from heaven by St Michael, he landed on Earth among a painful patch of brambles. Since then, in resentment towards both plant and saint, he spitefully despoils the blackberries on Michaelmas Day each year. However, many people choose to follow Old Michaelmas Day as the annual eat-by date (10th October), allowing an extra eleven days of picking from the purple patch!

The 14th September is designated as Holy Cross Day within the church calendar, also known as the Devil's Nutting Day. In folklore, this is the one day of the year to refrain from gathering hazelnuts as Old Nick is out and about; eager to harvest stray souls as well as nuts. Some say that good Christian folk shouldn't go nutting on any Sunday either in order to avoid an infernal encounter. A plant called Devil's-bit scabious is often still flowering in meadows and marshes during September – adding a welcome splash of colour against the fading fabric of the countryside. Traditionally, this plant was used as a treatment for skin irritations, such as scabies (hence the latter part of its name). It has a noticeably truncated root below ground that, according to legend, was once bitten off by the Devil himself to curtail the growth of such a helpful, healing plant to humanity.

Elder Witchery

As the evenings grow longer after the autumn equinox, strange shapes shift in the shadows. A well as mercurial white hares, witches are also believed to take the form of crooked, old elder trees. In contrast to the light, flowery nature of elder in June, the folklore and stories of elder in autumn are as dark and seductive as its fruit. One folk tale, collected by the Brothers Grimm, tells of a sinister sorceress who used her elemental magic to transform into an elder tree: toes delving deeply as roots, body twisting into a trunk, arms stretching wide as branches. There, she would wait in tree form for a passing traveller to rest against her trunk. Then, with a creaking of wood and scratching of flesh, they would be trapped in the eldern arms of the witch. Another West Country folk tale relates how a poor farmstead is terrorised each night by the scrabbling, scraping sounds of an elder witch with malicious intent. In the end, the creature is thwarted by the old granny of the house bravely opening the door and throwing out a shovelful of burning embers; turning the tree to cinders.

Elder is much mistrusted as a firewood: according to superstition, burning it inside the home will summon the Devil to come and dance on the chimney. Similarly, elder is rarely used in carpentry and its timber should only be taken by explicitly asking permission of the Elder Mother:

Owd girl, give me some of thy wood
And I'll give you some of mine,
When I grow into a tree ...

In contrast to tales of human characters using (or scapegoated for) witchcraft, such elder witches are 'elemental' in form – personifications of the death and darkness inherent to autumn.

Seeds of Change

When the autumn leaves are golden, when the evening air is chill,
When the swallows leave us for a place where there is summer still.

Harvey Andrews

The first Monday after Michaelmas is traditionally known as Pack Monday – a time for workers to pack up and move on from their employment. In some places it was called Pack and Penny Day, as a bonus payment was also given after a year's work. Pack Monday Fair is still celebrated in Sherborne, Dorset, but now falls in October; following the Old Calendar. September is also when the school year restarts in England and Wales, with the name Michaelmas still widely used for the first academic term. Michaelmas daisies (actually a culti- vated variety of aster) blossom around the end of September, providing a late flowery flourish in the garden. Traditionally they were given as gifts, especially to those leaving their home or job at this time of year, reflecting the sense of endings and beginnings seen in the natural world.

Far-flying swifts have mostly left by September, and our cherished swal- lows head south by the end of the month, taking the last of the warm weather with them. Chiffchaffs, silent in high summer, pipe up again in autumn; reprising their spring song before they disappear, too. In woods, waysides and parks, the trees drop their seeds: ash keys, acorns and the spinning seeds of sycamore and maple. Practically speaking, now is a good time for scattering wild flower seeds for next year's summer meadows. It's also an inspiring sea- sonal moment for us to let go of past concerns and make new plans – sowing seeds for the future.

All the flowers of tomorrow are in the seeds of today.

Old Roots, New Shoots

MOON WALKING

We might no longer need to *work* by the light of a Harvest Moon, but it provides a heaven-sent opportunity to go out for a *walk* beneath its benign illumination. September evenings can be soft and sensual; still mild but with the first tinges of autumnal freshness. The transcendent moonlight changes familiar landscapes into fresh vistas where we can, literally, see things in a different light. Avoid using a torch, as it takes the eyes a while to adjust from artificial light to moon-vision. A moon walk is also a good way to encounter the 'other world' of nature: the scent of a fox, the screech of an owl, the singing of crickets or the fluttering of ghostly moths. You might, perhaps, catch a flash of bright white fur, haring out of the stubble fields and into the darkness of the trees. At some point on the walk, it's worth stopping at a comfortable spot to lie down (take a picnic blanket) to savour the night sounds while gazing up at the moon, reflecting on its many myths and mysteries. A pair of binoculars brings a whole, other world of wonder into view. If you're very lucky you might catch sight of a pale, pearlescent 'moonbow' – a lunar rainbow, caused by the bright light of a full moon refracted through heavy moisture in the air at this time of year.

10

October

O'er the wall in the churchyard the apple trees lean
And ripen their burdens: red, yellow and green.
In autumn the apples among the graves lie;
'There I'll sleep well,' says Uncle, when fated to die.

Lazy Lawrence

Once there was a name that anyone who's ever scrumped for apples in the West Country used to know – *Lazy Lawrence*. He's the pixie pony, the faerie horse, the sprightly sprite of a stallion who gallops around the orchards guarding the apple trees and protecting their juicy treasures in autumn. They call him Lazy Lawrence, but that doesn't tell the story – he's as wild and feisty and free as the west wind, and woe betide anyone out and about in an orchard picking other people's apples. For Lazy Lawrence could give a nasty nip with his teeth or a cracking kick with his hooves, and anyone caught in the glare of his green eyes would be transfixed, rooted to the spot, unable to move a muscle except to cry, 'Lazy Lawrence let me go, don't hold me winter and summer too!'

Well, in a little village on the Somerset–Dorset border, there once lived an old farmer's widow who owned an old apple orchard. It was a wild and wonderful place, filled with gnarled, old trees that each year produced an abundance of apples: apples for eating, apples for keeping, apples for cooking and apples for turning into cider. She was a woman who followed the Old Ways and didn't forget to look after the otherworldly orchard denizen. Every evening she left a bucket of clear water and a dish of oats and cream under the trees for Lazy Lawrence. And sure enough, every morning, both bucket and bowl were empty.

Well, sad to say, the old woman had a nasty neighbour – a mean and miserable man, as sour as cider vinegar. Living alone in a dark house, he spent his time studying the dark arts, eventually becoming a powerful conjuror. One year, he looked across at the old widow's orchard of ripening fruit with jealous eyes, vowing to use his malicious magic to steal all her apples for himself. But he was no fool – he knew about Lazy Lawrence, so carefully made necessary preparations. He bought a huge wicker basket and wove into it spells of protection and levitation. Then, one cold, clear night in October, he climbed into the flying basket and sailed it across the starlit sky, landing in the middle of the old widow's orchard. There, using his sorcery, he stripped the apples from the trees and into the basket beneath him. Before long he'd stolen every last apple from every last tree in the orchard. All except one: a big Bramley that still clung stubbornly to the branch. But the mean magician was so selfish, and so spiteful, that he couldn't bear to leave the widow with even one apple. He multiplied his magical enchantments, straining with outstretched fingers, until eventually, with a crack, the apple snapped from its stalk. But it flew straight through the air and hit him hard in his left eye, sending him tumbling backwards out of the basket with a loud cry of pain. His cry was answered by a horse's whinny: there was Lazy Lawrence with flashing eyes and bared teeth. Round the orchard the conjurer was kicked and nipped until, turning to face the fairy horse, he was caught in the glare of his green eyes. Instantly he was transfixed, rooted to the spot, unable to do anything except cry out loud, 'Lazy Lawrence let me go, don't hold me winter and summer too!'

But Lazy Lawrence didn't let him go. The mean magician stayed in the cold orchard all night long, as stiff as a scarecrow. Finally, the morning sunshine broke the spell and he ran as fast as he could – out of the orchard and out of the village; never to be seen again. But when the old widow woke that morning, she found her apples already picked and packed in a big wicker basket. Then she saw the hoofprints underneath the trees and knew, with a grateful smile, that Lazy Lawrence had done his job.

Appley Ever After

October brings a final flourish to autumnal fruitfulness and the cherished apple now takes centre stage. In the orchard, this month marks the culmination of the harvest for dessert and cooking apples, and the start of the season for picking and pressing cider apples. All of which is actively celebrated every year through Apple Day, held on, or around, 21st October. It's a relatively new addition to the festive calendar, initiated by environmental arts charity Common Ground in 1990 as a new community celebration of autumn, specifically focussing on the diversity and distinctiveness of apples. The very first event was held at the site of an old costermongers' market in London, raising awareness of the wealth of traditional apple varieties and the importance of old orchards for both nature and culture. It quickly took root in the public imagination and nowadays is celebrated seasonally in every corner of the UK, as well as many other countries where apples are grown around the world.

Most Apple Day events take place outdoors among the trees themselves, including an increasing number of community orchards. The abundance of the orchard inspires a generosity of spirit at these festive occasions, with ample free tastings of apples, both raw and in all their various culinary incarnations: cakes, pies, toffee apples, juice and – of course – cider from last year's crop. Often there's an opportunity to sample a selection of different locally grown varieties, or have your own garden apple identified by an expert. Like the apple varieties themselves, each event is a particular expression of people and place. Common ingredients including music and morris dancing, singing and storytelling, as well as playfully competitive games, such as apple and spoon races, apple bobbing and longest apple peel competitions. In Bridport, Dorset, they perform an annual Apple Day mummers' play – with a guest appearance from Lazy Lawrence himself, in pantomime horse style.

There's nothing more English than an apple. And yet, many other countries say the same thing! France, Australia, South Africa and the USA all variously hold the apple as their own national treasure – it's as homely as apple pie. However, although crab apples are native to Britain, genetic research has shown that all domestic apple varieties trace their ancestry to one location: the Tien Shan valley in Kazakhstan. From there, along the Silk Road and Roman marching routes, apple trees have taken root around the world and grown into locally distinctive forms and varieties.

Fruit out of season, sounds out of reason.

In Britain, the West Country in particular, cider making starts in late October – customarily it's made at the waning of the year and the waxing of the moon. Recently, an increasing thirst for both locally made and artisan styles of drink has resulted in a revival in small-scale cider production, often using traditional skills and equipment. An old-fashioned cider barn is a magical place to be at this time of year, motes of straw dust catching shafts of slanting light as freshly milled apple pulp is heaped by many hands into a multi-storey stack, then stitched together with layers of farmyard straw. The resulting 'cheese' is then ready to be gently squeezed, as a big beam of old oak is slowly screwed down-wards from above. The fresh juice, bright orange and sweet smelling, gushes, then trickles into the collecting vessel. Time to wipe brows and rehydrate: the last barrel of old cider is drained to make way for its new occupant; while rais-ing a toast to the orchard and the fine flavour of its fermented fruits.

The end of the month is apple flavoured, too. The 31st October is known as Allantide – the eve of Saint Allan's Day – when, in Cornwall in particular, highly polished red apples were offered as gifts for friends and family. These seasonally abundant fruits have featured in traditional games at this time of year, long before Apple Day itself had even set seed. The familiar custom of apple bobbing – where players try to grab apples floating in a bowl of water (or suspended from a string) using only their mouths – was once common at Hallowe'en and is thought to have originated with the Romans. The game was associated with love and fertility, attributes of the Roman goddess Pomona (see below). In Ireland the game is called Snap Apple, where 31st October is also known as Snap Apple Night.

That Old Chestnut

Sweet chestnuts also come to fruition in October, one of the last wild harvests of the year, providing a tasty treat when toasted on the fire as the evenings turn chilly. They are easily gathered from beneath trees, with their spikey hedgehog cases partly split open to reveal a glimpse of the shiny, brown treasures within. Horse chestnuts (not related, except by common name) are also gathered during this month – not suitable for consumption, but gainfully employed in the well-known, and well-loved, game of 'conkers'. Playing is a simple contest between two people taking turns to smash each other's conker suspended on a string. However, playing prowess is afforded great status, with the annual World Conker Championships held in the village of Ashton, Northamptonshire, on the second Sunday of October. The competition allegedly originated in 1965 when two anglers resorted to alternative amusement after a cancelled fishing trip. Old folk-lore holds that placing conkers around the house will keep spiders away.

Good God!

This time of year has long been held as an auspicious season to commune with the gods – giving thanks for the end of the agricultural year and pleading for protection during the dark days ahead. Gathering together with a toast of mead, ale or cider was, and perhaps still is, believed to be a good way to enter into a heavenly state of mind. The Celtic god Dagda was honoured at this time of year, whose name translates as 'good god'. Like Lugh, celebrated in August, he was a leader of the mythical Tuatha Dé Danann in Ireland and is associated with wisdom as well as having weather-related powers. In myth, he possesses several magical items with strong seasonal relevance: a never-empty cauldron of food, ever-fruiting apple trees, a club that both killed and brought back to life and a golden-stringed harp, whose music controlled both the Earth's climate and human emotions.

In Roman mythology, the god Vertumnus (whose name is a fusion of vernal and autumnal) is also famed for supernatural control over the seasons and plant growth, as well as being able to change shape at will. According to one legend, after falling in love with Pomona, the goddess of fruitfulness, he tricks his way into her sacred apple orchard by disguising himself as an old woman. His deception was given away, too late, by his hot, sensuous kisses – ill-fitting of an old hag! The narrative of gaining entry to a sacred orchard through mischief and dark sorcery is also echoed in the Lazy Lawrence folk tale above.

Summer's End

By the end of October, the fields are harvested and fallow, the livestock are brought back in from summer pastures, flowers have long since faded and fallen leaves form a thick layer on the ground. In the Celtic calendar, 31st October is celebrated as Samhain (usually pronounced sow-een), meaning 'summer's end'; marking the start of the dark half of the year. As with Beltane, at the exact opposite position on the wheel of the year, once more there's a strong sense of sacredness attached to being on the edge: between seasons, between two months, between night and day. In mythology, such creases in time have caused the boundaries between our world and other worlds to wear thin; like the folds on a well-used map. For pastoral societies where the wellbeing of livestock was dependent on seasonal changes, Samhain was both pregnant with possibility and fraught with fear. The fairy folk are said to be particularly active, and highly mischievous, at this time of year – travelling abroad was generally avoided for fear of being 'pixy-led'. In Ireland, 'pookas' are also prevalent – nefarious, shape-shifting spirits taking the form of humans or domestic animals, especially horses. Like Lazy Lawrence, the fairy horse of the orchard, they could bring either good tidings or ill fortune and it was wise to leave a small offering of food for them outside the house.

As with the other three main Celtic festivals, 'need fires' were ignited at Samhain – communal and ceremonial bonfires to brighten the darkness as the sun's fire was dwindling in the sky. Torches or lanterns would then be processed across the fields and brought back into homes, as the fires in the hearth were rekindled for the first time. It's a time to be warm and cosy by the hearth, telling tales. In Wales, this time of year is known as Nos Calan Gaeaf – the night before winter – and is also marked by gathering round bonfires. However, it's essential to be home before the flames die down, as Y Ladi Wen (the White Lady) appears in the darkness to take the souls of anyone lingering too long. The Anglo-Saxon name for October was Winterfylleth, meaning 'winter full moon', and also marking the beginning of the cold, dark half of the year. The traditional name for this month's full moon is Hunter's Moon: marking the season for pursuing larger game, such as deer, as woodlands lose their leafy cover and the radiant moon offers a helpful light to hunters.

Hallowed Times

Over the years, sacred rituals of protection and propitiation at summer's end have slowly become suffused with a sense of supernatural fears at the approach of winter. In terms of folklore, it's the twilight of the year, with all the dark magic and delicate mystery that comes with fading light and growing shadows. The 31st October is now widely known as Hallowe'en, its name stemming from All Hallows' Eve – the following day (1st November) being the feast of All Saints, with all the associations of death and ancestors explored in the next chapter. For many, it's also a time to relish lighting the dark nights with flickering candles, festive lanterns and carved pumpkins; or turnips as they once were.

Jack O' Lantern

Once, in Old Ireland, there was a blacksmith called Jack – a wicked and wayward character, with a soul as sooty as his blackened hands. He spent more time drinking and gambling in the pub than he ever did working in the smithy and, needless to say, was never seen in church. But Jack had a silver tongue and managed to fund his nefarious lifestyle by swindling unwary customers. His old neighbours shook their heads in disbelief, declaring he was so cunning that he could deceive the Devil himself. On hearing such stories, the Old Lad decided to pay Jack a visit.

One day in late autumn, as the wild wind blew big bunches of leaves from the trees, Old Nick caught up with Jack on his way to the pub. In a flash of inspiration, smooth-talking Jack persuaded the Devil that, rather than going down to the fiery furnaces, they should spend the evening together drinking. Fuelled by whiskey, the two of them were soon making merry, with much in common and plenty of devilish tales between them. The Devil was generous in buying drinks throughout the evening, recognising a kindred spirit, but by the end of the night it was Jack's turn to pay for the last round. Once more, he quickly conceived a cunning plan – telling the Devil to turn himself temporarily into a silver sixpence, to pay for the drinks and trick the landlord at the same time! The Old Lad was happy to play his part, delighting in finding someone as dishonest and devious as himself. But Jack quickly put the coin in his pocket, next to a silver crucifix, and the Devil was trapped by the holy power of the cross. In the end, the Devil offered Jack another decade of decadent life without interference, if he released him from his pocket.

After another ten years of even more wayward living, Old Scratch came back and found Jack in his garden, pruning the fruit trees. Before being taken down to hell, Jack begged the Devil to climb his tree and pick an apple – a last meal for a condemned man. The Old Feller obliged but then, quick as a fox, Jack carved the shape of the cross on the trunk with his billhook, once more trapping the Devil in the top of the tree. He roared in unholy rage, hurling horrible insults and pleading to be released.

'I'll let you free,' said Jack, 'if you promise to never, ever take me to hell.'

It was a hard bargain, but the deal was done. By now, however, Jack didn't have much span of life left: the very next year he died, on the last breath of October. Trying his luck, he made his way to the pearly gates, where Saint Peter shook his head in righteous disbelief – there could be no entry for a soul as stained as Jack's. Reluctantly, since he couldn't enter heaven, Jack made his way down to the gates of hell. With a sardonic smile, the Devil shook his horned head, reminding Jack of the promise in the apple tree. So, Jack was caught between heaven and hell, lost and lonely in a never-ending no-man's-land. In the end, out of both pity and admiration, Old Nick gave Jack a burning ember from the fires of hell. Unable to hold its heat in his hands, he hollowed out a turnip and put the flaming coal inside, making himself a little lantern. From that day on, Jack has wandered in the cold darkness, with just his infernal light to keep him company. So it is, at the end of October, when the veil between worlds is thin, his ghoulish lantern can still be seen meandering in the twilight. Since then, at Hallowe'en each year, people carve their own little lanterns from turnips, or other vegetables, to remember the cautionary tale of Jack O' Lantern.

Punkie Night

A similar, but more down to earth, story from Somerset offers an alternative origin for Hallowe'en lanterns. A group of men from the village of Hinton St George once went to visit a nearby autumn fair, but, having been overly familiar with the cider barrel, failed to return by nightfall. Eventually, the stout-hearted women folk of the village determined to go out and bring their men home. The night was dark and windy, so they made candle lanterns to find their way, carved from mangold worzels – a type of root vegetable colloquially called 'punkies'. The legendary piece of local history is still celebrated every year at the end of October as Punkie Night, with a costumed procession of families carrying punkie lanterns, singing the traditional song:

> It's Punkie Night tonight, it's Punkie Night tonight,
> Give us a candle, give us a light, it's Punkie Night tonight!

Fruits of Fortune

Hallowe'en, with all its supernatural associations, has long been used as a prime time for telling fortunes. Autumnal fruits provide a handy means of divination, namely apples and hazelnuts, which both symbolise fertility and abundance. Apple peel, removed in one long piece, was thrown over the shoulder at Hallowe'en to reveal the first letter of a future lover in its shape. Apple pips, placed by the burning hearth, are used for divining the devotion of potential lovers:

> If you love me, bounce and fly,
> If you hate me, lie and die.

Similarly, hazelnuts placed by the fire can be used to test the fidelity of proposed love matches: if they crack, it is an omen that so too will the relationship. For this reason, 31st October is also known as Nut-crack Night in some parts of England.

Mushroom Magic

Whilst most of the wild world dies down, there are strange stirrings at ground level. Across fields and forests in October, weird and wonderful growth forms suddenly appear, like magic: mushrooms and toadstools. These seasonally visible fruiting bodies are just the tip of the iceberg – the much larger mycelial mass of ghost-like fungal threads lies hidden underground. There, in the dark, they do the dirty work of decomposition, turning the remains of the old year into nutrients to fuel next year's new growth. Neither plant nor animal, they're a bridge between worlds; connecting the living and the dead in the so-called 'wood wide web'.

Many mushrooms are edible; many are not. Understanding the difference is a matter of life and death. But for those that properly know their business, an autumn harvest of foraged fungi provides a tasty and hearty feast. According to folklore, mushrooms are said to be best gathered by the light of a full moon. The Hunter's Moon rides in October and mushrooms make a delicious companion to wild game, also abounding in the woods. Fungi's importance as a food source is highlighted in a traditional Christian legend. God and Saint Peter were once walking together on Earth, discussing the affairs of humanity. As they sauntered through the ripe harvest fields, Peter absentmindedly picked and chewed on a stalk of rye, whereby God immediately rebuked him for taking food away from humanity. But, as Peter spat out the chewed cereals, edible mushrooms suddenly sprouted up in the same spot – God's blessing for all those in need of seasonal sustenance.

While science is only just beginning to uncover the mysteries of mycology, fungi have long been recognised as important and potent in mythology; with mushroom folklore particularly prevalent among the rich compost of Hallowe'en. Mushrooms are sometimes seen as portals between worlds, leading to the land of the dead or the dangerous delights of Faerie. The association with the underworld is highlighted by one of the many folk names for fungus: 'fingers of the dead'. A yellow fungus, which grows conspicuously on woody vegetation in hedgerows at this time of year, is known as 'fairy butter' or 'witch's butter'; definitely not good for spreading on toast. There is even a rare, and poisonous, mushroom called Jack O' Lantern, which glows faintly in the dark, like its legendary namesake. Fairy rings – formed by concentric circles of fungal growth – are infamously favoured by fairies for their revels. They are highly taboo to humans and anyone that dallies within a fairy ring risks falling into an enchanted sleep, or disappearing altogether.

The Fairy Ring

Two farm-working friends in rural Wales, Rhys and David, were once walking home by the light of a Hunter's Moon after an evening in the wild woods; their canvas bags bulging by their sides. Suddenly, Rhys stopped in his tracks, his head cocked to one side. 'Do you hear that music?!' he asked excitedly. David strained to hear, but his ears could only just pick out the faint strands of a lilting harp, as delicate as spiders' silk caught on the breeze. The magical music pulled the men irresistibly forward through the dark until they came to a grassy clearing among the trees. There they saw a perfect circle of mushrooms; pale and ghostly in the moonlight. The music was louder and faster now, although they saw no sign of who, or what, was making it. Rhys's body began to tremble and twitch. 'What a wonderful tune! I could dance all night to that …'

'Don't be a fool!' replied his friend. 'It's fairy music. No good ever comes from dancing with the Tylwyth Teg. Come away!' He clasped his hand over his own ears and turned away. But Rhys refused to leave, spellbound by the music, until he suddenly stepped forward into the fairy ring …

Having returned back to the village alone, David stayed late and drank deep in the tavern that night – his worries about Rhys eventually drowned in good ale. But the next day Rhys was still missing and didn't turn up for work at the farm the following day either. Soon questions were being asked and when David told his tale of the fairy ring, suspicions were raised against David himself. The old farmer, however, was a wise man; familiar with the ways of the Tylwyth Teg. He told David to take him to the exact spot where Rhys was last seen. That evening they arrived at the fairy ring, with the mushrooms glistening in the moonlight, but now all was completely still and silent. The old farmer carefully put his left foot just inside the edge of the circle, keeping his other foot safely outside the ring. 'Now, put your foot on mine, then listen and look again …'

Now David could clearly hear the wild and wonderful music once more, with lilting harps and furious fiddles playing a jolly jig. Within the circle he saw a host of the Fair Folk, small as children but with ancient faces and wisps of silvery white hair, flying free as they danced together holding hands in a circle. Between the frolicking fairies was Rhys himself being led a merry dance, but clearly against his will. His body and legs were strangely angular and jerky, his face was ashen grey and contorted in a grim expression. The fairies seemed unaware of the two men observing, so the farmer patiently waited for the dancing circle to bring Rhys round to where they stood. Then, leaning forward as far as he could, without stepping fully inside the fairy ring, he grabbed Rhys by his tunic. With David also pulling from behind, together they managed to fling Rhys out of the ring. The music instantly stopped and the moon was quickly covered with dark clouds. Rhys lay on his back on the grass with wide, wild eyes. 'The music, bring back the music!' he cried over and over again.

David and the farmer had to forcefully drag Rhys away from the fairy ring, then they took him home to his bed. There he stayed, day and night, unmoving but unsleeping, slowly becoming weaker and more listless. Eventually, with the passing of autumn into winter, he died. Not everyone believed the story, of course, but those that went to find the fairy ring said the grass was bright green and lush where the mushrooms once grew – with the imprints of little feet clearly visible across the verdant turf.

Flavour of the Month

Poached Arctic Char, Apple Butter, Mushroom Powder and Bannock Bread

The time of year around Apple Day is also bliss for the seeker of fungi. With plenty of guidebooks, and a willingness to learn, you can begin to navigate around this vast topic for culinary gain. One can quickly learn to identify the ten safe fungi and, most importantly, the seven lethal ones in the UK.

Often overlooked, the hedgehog fungus (*Hydnum repandum*) is abundant during early October, in woodlands with sweet chestnut, western hemlock and holly – perfect for the 'in training' fungi forager. It's a pale white to cream mushroom that grows from the soil, with spines rather than gills, similar looking to those on its namesake. Eventually, you may happen upon a haul of 'hedgehogs' to create a valuable kitchen condiment – dried mushroom powder, a fantastic finish for all manner of dishes.

This supper recipe is manna for the soul, with Arctic char poached in apple juice and the apple liquor making the sauce, finished with mushroom powder for seasoning and bannock bread for mopping up it all up. Serves four.

MUSHROOM POWDER

    10g dried hedgehog fungi (or porcini/wild mushroom mix)
    2g salt
    1g citric acid

– Blend all ingredients to fine powder and store in airtight jars.

BANNOCK BREAD

Make one hour ahead of dinner in a 12in cast iron skillet, pre-heated over a low to medium heat.

    175g coarse oatmeal
    125g plain flour
    1 tsp bicarbonate of soda
    1 tsp fine sea salt
    175g buttermilk
    25g melted butter

- Add all the ingredients, except the buttermilk, to a mixing bowl and combine well. Add the buttermilk gradually, bringing the mix together without over-working the dough. Don't mix all the buttermilk in if not needed.
- Press the dough into a 1-inch thick piece around the same size as your cast iron pan and cook, only turning once to brown the top of the bannock.
- Allow to stand in the pan's residual heat until the other ingredients come together.

A fillet of Arctic char (approx. 700g)
Apple juice
Water
125g salted butter cubed

- Divide the fish fillet into four even-sized pieces. Poach the fish in a small pan with equal parts water and apple juice, just enough to cover the fillets.
- Set the cooked fillets aside somewhere warm.
- Reduce the cooking liquor over a fast heat, down to a mere teaspoon.
- Off the heat, whisk in a few cubes of the butter to create an emulsion.
- Add the remaining butter and whisk that in too, returning to the heat briefly if needed. The butter should remain emulsified and have splendid flavours from the reduced fish and apple stock.

St Luke's Summer

Brown-leaved fruits are turning red,
With golden sunshine overhead.

William Barnes

St Luke's Day is celebrated on 18th October and, despite chilly nights and damp mornings, there is often a period of calm, dry and sunny days around this time, known colloquially as 'St Luke's little summer'. St Luke is the patron of artists and in a spell of late-season sunshine, the natural world dazzles as a painter's palette of colours: burnished bronze, glittering gold and raucous reds. The warm sunshine also brings out bees, and other flying insects, for a final forage on ivy flowers – one of the few native plants to subvert the seasons, by blossoming in autumn and fruiting in spring.

Old Roots, New Shoots

A WALK IN THE WOODS

As autumn trees perform their annual striptease, the falling leaves gather on the ground below in a multi-coloured magic carpet. It's the perfect time of year to go for a wild walk in your neck of the woods to revel in the sensations of the season. Beech woods, in particular, form deep layers of leaves, perfect for wading through and reviving a moment of child-like autumnal glee. Among the woodland natives, we might happen across a 'wilding' apple tree – sprung up from a discarded core. It's worth reaching for a couple of fruits from the branch: take a bite, then take it to your local Apple Day; it might be a unique variety – the next 'big apple'.

October is the premier time to go looking for woodland mushrooms, as they emerge among the leaf litter, often after heavy rainstorms. There's an amazing variety of colours and shapes, with evocative names to match: glistening white porcelain fungus, spiky-gilled hedgehog fungus and cheeky-looking scarlet elf caps; left on dead twigs by the Little People to remind us of their invisible presence. Fungi provide a fine feast for the eyes, enjoyed wherever and whenever they appear in the woods. However, the names of other species – penny buns, beefsteak fungus and chicken of the woods – hint also at their hidden flavours. To take mushroom appreciation a step further, there are many 'fungal forays' led by local experts through autumn, providing a fascinating (and fatality-free) introduction to their identification and culinary potential.

Finally, the fierce bellowing of rutting stags can sometimes be heard echoing between the trees in October, as rival males strut their stuff to prove their procreative potential. It's a stunning spectacle; if enjoyed from a safe distance. In Norse mythology, four stags run around the Tree of Life, in an endless procession of the seasons. Now, with their stamping hooves and steaming breath in the chilled air, we know that winter's on its way.

11

November

It fell upon the Martinmas time,
When the snow lay on the border,
There came a troop of soldiers here
To take up their winter quarters.

The Dead Moon

In the dark half of the year when the sun sets sooner, and the dark part of the month when the moon is frail and thin, then dread things abound, making mischief for those who stray into the shadows. Once, the Lincolnshire fens were riddled with marshes and mires and seethed with slow, seeping water. To travel during the day was difficult enough but by night is was only safe to cross the marshland when the moon was bright and full. The gentle, generous moon, looking down from her celestial setting, grieved that fen folk suffered cruelly when her radiant face was turned away. In the end, she decided to try and help. She wrapped her luminous form in a night-black shawl, pulled its hood around her head, then stepped down from the heavens.

Down on Earth it was all soft and soggy, with swampy ground and perilous pools. The only visible light was her own pale luminescence that slipped out from the folds of her shawl as she tiptoed through the fens. As she journeyed deeper into the marshland, all manner of malignant and malicious beings teemed around her: bogles and boggarts, goblins and ghosts, hags and hunky-punks, witches and will-o'-wisps, growling black dogs and prowling cats with green-glowing eyes. The undead rose up from the watery graves with unblinking eyes and pallid, putrid fingers ready to snatch and strangle. The moon, light as light itself, avoided them all by stepping nimbly from tussock to tussock, and dry stone to dry stone. But then, suddenly, she heard a frantic splashing from one of the nearby pools – there she saw a lost traveller, floundering in the dark and treacherous water. Wanting to help, she pulled back the hem of her robe, allowing a little of her light to spill out – enough to illuminate a way out for the poor man before the foul fiends could ensnare him. Eyes wide with horror, he ran back along the path as fast as his feet could carry him.

But, as the moon readjusted her dark garments, her hood caught on the dead branch of an old sallow tree. As she twisted her body to free herself, a bony hand grabbed her by the waist and pulled her down to the damp ground. Now, unable to show her face or shine her light, the foul creatures crept closer; shrieks of jubilant laughter ringing out in the cold, claggy air. Gleefully they saw their opportunity to bury the moon, deep down, where her brightness would never again disturb their nightly reign of terror. Icy fingers held her in the water as a huge, hairy boggart rolled a flat stone over her helpless body. There she lay: lifeless, yet undying, in a cold, watery grave.

Dark times. The fen folk anxiously looked to the sky for the first silver sliver of the new moon. But it never came; only dark night after dark night. And in the darkness, foul air seeped out from the marshes, like the breath of death. The villagers locked their doors and stayed in their houses; trembling at the sounds of paddling feet and the gurgle of laughter outside. In the end, some of them braved the darkness to seek the help of the Old One in her turf-roofed cottage at the edge of the village. As they sat huddled together by her smouldering fire, she peered into an old, iron pot and flicked through the pages of a dusty, leather-bound book. All too clearly, she divined that the moon was lost to them, dead in the darkness. But even the Old One couldn't quite see exactly where she was hidden. Then one of the men by the fire suddenly spoke up: telling a tale he'd not thought to mention before. A few weeks ago, he'd been travelling home at night across the marsh but missed the track and fallen foul of a deep mire. He remembered seeing a sudden shimmering light that helped him find his way out of the bog and back to the path. 'It must have been the poor, old moon helping me, before she was caught by those foul fiends. I reckon I can still remember the place where it all happened …'

The eyes of the Old One flickered in the firelight: 'Then there's a chance to bring the moon back, if any dare take it?' Four heads nodded, slowly and solemnly, in the shadows. She warned them to carry hazel wands in their pockets and on no account open their mouths while in the marshland. Then she told them to retrace the traveller's footsteps and look for three signs: a candle, a cross and a coffin, that would reveal the spot where the moon was buried. Holding candle lanterns aloft, the four went into the swamp, shuddering at the slurping water and hissing whispers in the reeds. Like the moon before them, they stepped carefully from tussock to stone; eyes as wide as saucers. Then they saw a flickering light ahead of them, hovering just above the ground – like a candle. Screwing up their courage, they stepped towards it until they saw the withered branches of a sallow tree, unnaturally bent across each other – in the shape of a cross. Finally, peering down at the ground beneath the tree, they saw a long, flat stone – the size and shape of a coffin. This was it: a candle, a cross and a coffin!

Keeping their mouths firmly shut, with hazel wands safely inside their pockets, they began to heave the cold, grey stone with all their strength. As it slid aside, the men peered into the pool and saw a pale, beautiful face staring straight back at them. In a moment of mercurial energy, the moon leapt up and out from her grave, while drawing back her dark-hooded robe. For a moment her light was incandescent – swiftly sending the foul fiends scuttling away into the darkest shadows. Then the moon smiled brightly in gratitude to her rescuers, lighting their way home, before stepping up to her rightful setting in the night sky. From that time onwards, when the moon is full or waxing gibbous, she saves her brightest light for the darkest, dampest places – looking after her dear friends in the fens.

Lost Souls

The 1st November is marked as All Saints' Day in the church calendar – sometimes known as Hallowmas or Hollantide. The night before is All Hallows' Eve, giving rise to the very familiar phrase: Hallowe'en. The following day (2nd November) is All Souls' Day, and together these two feast days hold a sacred season for honouring those that have passed away. On the night of All Soul's Eve the dead were widely believed to visit their former homes, so relatives lit small fires outdoors, called 'tindles', and placed candles by windows to guide them home. Inside the house, offerings of food and drink were left at the table; a feast for the dead. More recently, such indigenous traditions have gained new resonance through festivals from other parts of the world that celebrate ancestors at this time of year – most notably the Day of the Dead in Mexico. The seasonal theme of honouring the dead has also accrued extra poignance, over the last century, through commemorating the fallen during two devastating world wars. Remembrance Sunday, for those who gave the ultimate sacrifice, is on the Sunday closest to Armistice Day (11th November).

All Saints/Souls overlaps with many of last month's Samhain traditions, marking the start of the darkest quarter of the seasonal calendar and a time of dying down in the natural world. All Souls' Day was traditionally the last date for bringing animals in from seasonal grazing pastures, ringing the death knell of summer for pastoral communities. Culturally, it resonates as the time for facing demons and peering into shadows; telling dark tales of the unearthly and the supernatural, such as the Wild Hunt story later in this chapter. Nowadays, we still delight in having our imaginations haunted by stories of ghosts and ghouls, albeit in the safety and comfort of our own homes. However, many folk tales, like The Dead Moon, also provide timely reassurance at this time of year that monsters can be beaten and that the moon will rise again from her dark grave. As the fen folk knew well, seasonal superstitions are invoked in order to avert malign influences; hazel wands in our pockets. In the Devon village of Shebbear, for instance, local residents still gather every year on 5th November to turn over a large boulder called the Devil's Stone, in order to prevent diabolical deeds befalling the village.

Soul Food

A soul cake, a soul cake,
Please good missus a soul cake!
An apple, a pear, a plum or a cherry,
Any good thing to make us all merry.

Remembering the dead was not just a solemn affair. In medieval Britain, one of the most prevalent practices for All Souls' Day was giving away 'soul-cakes' – edible gifts to both commemorate the dead and gain spiritual prestige for the benefactor. Soul cakes are traditionally made from flour and dried fruit, often flavoured with various spices such as nutmeg, ginger and cinnamon – sweet treats during dark days. These seasonal bakes also gave rise to a custom called 'souling', where groups of children, or needy parishioners, would go visiting from house to house singing songs in return for cakes, fruits or other goodies.

Visiting houses, both public and private, to sing for your supper has lots in common with other winter festivities, such as wassailing (see January) and later 'penny for the guy' traditions around Bonfire Night. Soul Plays, a season-

ally specific form of mummers' play (see December), were widely performed during the first days of November and have been enthusiastically revived in some places. The Antrobus Soul Play, in Cheshire, famously features a dead horse, called Dick Tatton:

> He once was alive but now he's dead,
> He's nothing but a poor old horse's head ...

Wearing disguises was commonplace for those going a-souling – perhaps a precursor to costumed 'trick or treat' activities in modern-day Hallowe'en. Another such precursor is the aptly named Mischief Night, when children were afforded free rein to play tricks on adults. At some point in time the tradition seems to have moved from May Day Eve to this dark, devilish time of year; becoming associated with both All Hallows and Bonfire Night.

Fire, Fire!

> Remember, remember! The fifth of November,
> The gunpowder, treason and plot.

The 5th November is the well-known annual commemoration of the Gunpowder Plot, when Guy Fawkes was foiled in his attempt to blow up the Houses of Parliament in 1605. It now pulls together a host of fiery celebrations; in both substance and spirit. Many places celebrate Bonfire Night, in Britain and beyond, but the Sussex town of Lewes burns brightly with its annual fireworks and is rightly acclaimed as the bonfire capital of the world. There are twenty-five to thirty separate bonfire societies that congregate on the 5th November in various locations across town, with costumed processions, fireworks displays and large-scale bonfires. As well as Guy's explosive exploits, the Lewes events also commemorate the burning at the stake of several local protestant martyrs during the reign of Mary Tudor; with seventeen burning crosses paraded through the town. The riotous festivities have been challenged by various authorities over the years, but the town defiantly continues with its fiery acts of rebellion, including burning effigies of reviled prominent characters from both past and present.

Smaller scale, but equally passionate, is a rowdy seasonal celebration called the Tar Barrels of Ottery St Mary, which takes place in the otherwise sleepy Devon town on 5th November. Through the evening, a series of flaming barrels are lit outside each of the town's many pubs and then hoisted onto the shoulders of specially nominated locals. The blazing barrels are then hauled, with surprising speed and perilous precariousness, through the crowded streets; as the smell of burning tar and sound of shrieking spectators fills the night air. Eventually, just before it's completely burnt through, each barrel is thrown to the ground in a final explosion of flames, sparks and embers. Given the considerable health and safety measures now required, it's a testament to the strength of local feeling that this living tradition continues to light up the night each year.

Flavour of the Month

Venison Skewers, Whole-Roast Crown Prince Squash & Hedgerow Ketchup

Gathering by the fireside in the evening chill is always better with food, and the season holds some great ingredients that cook wonderfully on open embers. One we look forward to every year is the mighty crown prince – a light blue-green squash with dense nutritious flesh and enough body to cook directly on coals. The flesh inside will steam, and its flavour concentrate. The season is also rich in wild game: birds, fish and deer; their addition to open-fire cooking can be very welcoming even in small amounts. A peek into the freezer can be rewarding, as we have an excellent use for bilberries and other wild fruits gathered in August and September: hedgerow ketchup, deep purple and glossy, with a hint of fire from chipotle chillies, as a marinade for venison steaks.

HEDGEROW KETCHUP
Makes about 400ml

800g mix of bilberry/elderberry/blackberry/hawthorn – whatever you can find in the freezer
250g apple cider vinegar
250g muscovado sugar
One cinnamon stick
Two dried chipotle chillies
1 tsp black peppercorns
1½ teaspoons fine sea salt

- Crush the black pepper and chillies in a pestle and mortar.
- Heat the cider vinegar, chillies and crushed pepper in a pan.
- Add the fruit mixture and salt and simmer gently for twenty to twenty-five minutes, until everything is softened.
- To remove the pulp, push the mixture through a sieve over another pan, with the aid of a spatula.
- Add the muscovado sugar to the liquor and hard boil for eight to ten minutes until it resembles the consistency of your favourite shop-bought condiment.
- Place in a sterilised jar and, once cooled, refrigerate for up to a week.

VENISON SKEWERS
 400g venison haunch steak
 20g molasses
 5g Marmite
 30ml Worcestershire sauce
 5g salt
 Olive oil

- Marinate the venison steak in the morning to let the acidity tenderise the meat and take on the flavours.
- Mix the oil, molasses, Marmite, and salt in a bowl using the Worcestershire sauce to loosen the marinade to a syrup consistency.
- Cube the venison haunch steaks to square, even 2cm cubes, and combine into the marinade. Thread the venison skewers and refrigerate covered until fire time; serves four.
- Cook your squash directly on well burned down embers. Allow at least an hour, quarter turning every fifteen minutes or so until the body has a give and the skin is well golden to charred.
- When the squash is nearly ready, cook the venison skewers until lightly caramelised.
- Plate together, serve with hedgerow ketchup and enjoy this primitive cookery post haste. It really can't be bettered.

Fresh Blood

The 11th November is St Martin's Day in the Christian calendar, better known as Martinmas. Traditionally, it's a time for forecasting the winter weather:

> If Martinmas ice will bear a duck,
> The rest of winter will be mire and muck.
> If leaves fall not by Martinmas Day,
> A cruel winter's on its way.

Martin de Tours was a fourth-century Roman soldier who, after converting to Christianity, renounced violence and founded a monastery on his way to sainthood. Ironically, for such a virtuous character, he purportedly shares his feast day with one of the annual festivals of Bacchus – the Roman god of drinking, dancing and debauchery. In Roman times, this was also the time when that year's new wine was first drawn; another cause for consumption and celebration. Both Bacchus and his ancient Greek counterpart Dionysus, were sometimes portrayed as virile bulls; which were sacrificially killed in their honour. In some northern European traditions, the sun itself is symbolised as a bull, killed at the onset of winter but providing ongoing sustenance in the form of meat. Ironically, according to legend, St Martin himself eventually died having taken the form of an ox. The seemingly uneasy mix of pious and pagan has nevertheless become neatly woven together in Britain as the first, blood-soaked, seasonal celebration of winter.

The Anglo-Saxon name for November was Blotmonath, which means 'blood month' or 'the month of sacrifice'. Martinmas itself became a time of year when the first of the livestock, fattened on summer pastures, were ceremonially killed. This served as both a celebratory feast of fresh meat at the end of the farming year and an act of religious propitiation, with some of the animal blood sprinkled on household thresholds to invoke divine protection. The by-products of butchery were then stored as salted, dried or smoked meat (including a cured recipe known as Martinmas beef), to help stave off the cold days and dark nights ahead, just as other seasonal foods were dwindling. Rural rituals eventually led to communal merrymaking and in medieval times Martinmas was much loved as a national holiday in Britain – a relished occasion for feasting and festivities in an otherwise austere time of year. As with Michaelmas in September, several other seasonal customs were tied to Martinmas, e.g. payment of annual rents or 'cattle money'.

Out Foxed

The fox went out on a chilly night,
He prayed for the moon to give him light ...

With autumnal auburn fur, flecked with winter whites and blacks, foxes seem to be the embodiment of seasonal colour at this time of year. In November, young males disperse from their home territories and can be frequently seen ranging across town and country, seeking food, territories and wild adventures. The fox is deeply entwined within human culture in Britain and Ireland, peering out of hundreds of folk tales and songs. The old English word for a fox is Tod, made famous by Beatrix Potter's tale of that name. A later, and more commonly known folk name is Reynard, based on Old French and German and meaning 'strong counsel'. The name was popularised in a twelfth-century text *The History of Reynard the Fox*, with its series of adventures about the anthropomorphic protagonist besting other animals; reminiscent of Roald Dahl's *Fantastic Mr Fox*. From Brer Fox to Aesop's Fables, fox is portrayed as a trickster: sly and cunning and capable of great charm to hide his rapacious animal instincts. A traditional English folk song, called Reynardine, describes a man with a distinctly vulpine nature leading a beautiful young woman to his den:

Sun and dark she followed him, his teeth did brightly shine.
And he led her up a-the mountains, did that sly, bold Reynardine!

In a similar, and even darker, folk tale, the eponymous 'Mr Fox' is a sly aristocrat who stalks and murders a series of young women, until his eventual comeuppance by a plucky heroine.

Yet the same sly fox is also adaptable and resourceful – seemingly able to shift in and out of territories and time zones. In other traditional folk tales, foxes (often vixens) are portrayed as human helpers – appearing, like magic, when all else is lost. One Scottish story tells of a kindly old woman who finds herself in a winter lockdown: trapped in her own house by heavy snowfall outside. The only way she survives her enforced isolation is through the morsels of meat that a fox drops down her chimney. Foxes, somewhere between domestic dogs and wild wolves, provide a cultural connection between the human and the more-than-human worlds; a link to the wildness within ourselves. Watching a fox delicately stepping out across the stubble fields at dusk, it's impossible not to admire how supremely attuned they are to the natural world. However, to walk past a fox's den in early winter is to be assaulted by an intense, earthy smell; almost unbearable.

Fox Skin

One evening, in the owl light, a woodcutter was returning home to his cabin in the woods, where he lived alone. Suddenly, he froze: he could see smoke rising up from the chimney – someone else was in the house! But as he opened the door, a delicious smell of simmering stew wafted out. Standing by the fire was a young woman, with long, auburn hair falling down her shoulders. Turning around, she looked at him with lively, hazel eyes and said that she'd come to be his wife – if he wanted. Her only condition was that her fox-skin coat must always stay hanging on the door, inside the house. The hunter happily consented. Soon the two of them were sharing a life together, shifting through the seasons. While he was felling trees in the forest, she was out hunting wild game. Each night when he returned the pot was bubbling with a hearty, meaty stew.

Eventually, however, the heady scent of her fox skin hanging on the door began to bother the woodcutter. Sometimes, especially in autumn, it released a pungent, musky odour; damp earth and dead things. As the weeks went by the smell intensified, suffusing the air of the cabin and seeping into his dreams. Suddenly, one winter's morning, he impulsively grabbed the coat and threw it out of the cabin. There was a high-pitched yelp as his wife jumped to her feet and ran out of the open door, pausing only to pick up her pelt. In a flurry of fur and the twitch of a tail, she transformed back into the shape of a fox and disappeared into the wild woods.

The Wild Hunt

An alternative Anglo-Saxon name for November was Wint-monath – 'wind month'. As with March, the other wild month, storm clouds and gusty winds are commonplace at this time of year – sometimes carrying the haunting sound of a hunting horn. Ancient in origin, capricious in nature and varied in its geographical appearances, the Wild Hunt continues to capture the imagination. Although sometimes associated with Yuletide, it incorporates seasonal symbolism, ancestor worship and echoes of bloody battles, all of which fit well with the wild weather and dark traditions of November.

> My hide unto the Huntsman, so freely I would give,
> My body to the hounds, for I'd rather die than live.

The Wild Hunt is always led by a spectral huntsman, taking many names and guises across time and place: Odin in the north, Herne in the south, Wild Edric in the west, Gwynn ap Nudd (ruler of the Otherworld) in Wales and the Devil wherever he pleases. The ever-attendant pack of hellhounds also take many names: Wisht Hounds, Yeth Hounds or the Devil's Dandy Dogs, and, according to some legends, they are phantom incarnations of deceased babies. Wherever the Huntsman turns his black horse, the baying hounds follow – their main prey being unwary travellers and unbaptised souls of the recently dead. To witness the passage of the Wild Hunt is most unwise and said to foreshadow horrible happenings for both the observer and the local area. In one particularly gruesome tale from Dartmoor (the Wild Hunt often manifests in that legendary landscape), a foolish farmer dares to ask the Huntsman what quarry he has captured. In reply, a heavily wrapped bundle is thrown to the ground at his feet – the farmer is mortified to discover it contains the body of his own child. Worse still, arrogant or ill-spoken words can result in being pressed into joining the Wild Hunt, in an undying but enduring torment.

The Black Fox

Once there was a priest named Dando who was living in the parish of Tavistock, on the edge of Dartmoor. Although ostensibly a man of the cloth, he was utterly stained with sin; the older he got the more deeply dyed he became from the dark waters in which he chose to wallow. Not least of his many vices was arrogance, being most proud and pompous about his skill as a huntsman. Dando spent much of his plentiful free time scouring the county in search of good sport from the saddle of his high horse. In particular he loved to hunt wily foxes, and in pursuit of such he gave no heed to property or propriety; nor the damage his horse's hooves left behind.

One dreary Sunday in November, after performing his perfunctory duties in church, he heard that a black fox had recently been spotted on the moorland near Crockern Tor. Here was a quarry worthy of his skill and, despite it still being the Sabbath, Dando was soon sat astride his best horse, a dapple grey mare, with three hunting hounds running ahead. The weather was foul that day and the further he rode, the wilder the wind blew and the darker the day became. The dogs caught no scent of a trail, and he no sight of a fox's tail, so after a several fruitless hours, Dando's demeanour was as stormy as the weather. But his pride would not allow himself to give up. He spurred his horse and harried his hounds across the moor without relent, until suddenly he saw the dark silhouette of another rider, standing proud on Crockern Tor. Thinking he must also be hunting the same black fox, Dando urged his horse up the steep, stony flanks to join the stranger; arriving breathless at the summit. The rider was dressed impeccably in a pitch-black hunting suit and top hat, with darkly glinting eyes. He immediately offered a drink from his hip flask, which Dando gladly accepted. The liquor felt like liquid fire as he greedily gulped it down.

'Hellishly good! What on Earth is it?'

'Nothing on Earth,' replied the black rider as a slight smile slid across his face. Dando's horse instinctively edged backwards and the dogs cowered to the ground, snivelling.

Dando tugged hard on his horse's reins. 'Have you seen a black fox? It's eluded me all day, and I'd ride to hell in order to catch the blasted beast.'

'So be it. Follow me!'

The mysterious huntsman spurred his horse and suddenly the sound of baying hounds filled the air. A large pack of black dogs came swarming over the tor; red tongues lolling and yellow eyes flashing. Dando followed as fast as he could behind the relentless huntsman and his hounds. The course they took crossed several streams, where Dando watched in amazement as steam hissed from the black stallion's hooves. Eventually they approached the shadowy features of Wistman's Wood and, without hesitation, the huntsman and his pack plunged into the twisted trees.

'What the Devil is he doing?!' Dando shouted out loud. 'No one can ride in that dense thicket.'

But just then he saw a fox, as black as coal save for a red tip on the end of its tail, come leaping out from the woods and out across the moor. 'At last! I'll have that infernal creature now ...'

Dando rode as hard as he could, but the fox was fleet of foot and unerring in its sense of direction. Beyond the trees the wild weather became a full-blown storm – lightning flashed across the dark sky and thunder rumbled heavily. Frightened for the first time, Dando suddenly found himself surrounded by the hellhounds – they harried his horse's legs and hurried him along. He was helplessly out of control by the time he saw the great gaping chasm in the ground in front of him, swirling with smoke and glowing fiery red from deep within. The fox and hounds ran straight into the hell hole, and Dando plunged after them. He was never seen, alive, again. But many Dartmoor folk have seen the Wild Hunt on winter nights since then. Some say that instead of Old Dewer on his black stallion, the hunt is now led by a ghastly, pale-faced rider on a dapple grey mare: Dando and his dogs.

Saints Above

Just as November begins with a bang, there are several saints' days at the end of the month with incendiary celebrations. In the church calendar the 3rd November is the feast day of St Clementine, the patron saint of blacksmiths, when fireworks and bangers were set off from old anvils outside forges. The story behind the custom tells that King Alfred, when asked which skilled trade was paramount, chose the tailor rather than the blacksmith. However, after an intervention from St Clementine himself, involving an anvil being knocked over in a shower of sparks, the King reversed his decision. The tradition has recently been revived, for instance at Finch Forge in Devon. Effigies of Old Clem were once paraded through villages on this day to allow children to go 'clementing' (begging for sweet treats); echoing the souling traditions earlier in the month.

The last day of the month (30th November) is the feast day of St Andrew, best known as the patron saint of Scotland. According to ancient legend, the help of the Apostle was received on the eve of a battle with invading Angles, after seeing the form of a white cross against the blue sky – the saltire of St Andrew. Perhaps reflecting his origins by the Sea of Galilee, he is also the patron saint of fishermen and is particularly revered in Scottish coastal towns, including St Andrews itself. Since 2006, St Andrew's Day has become an official national holiday in Scotland.

Old Roots, New Shoots

KEEPING THE FLAMES ALIVE

November is often perceived as the gloomiest of months, with leaden skies and lifeless landscapes. However, what it lacks in bright weather it more than makes up for with all its fiery traditions. This is the perfect time to have a garden bonfire – to burn away all the dead wood and gather around the flickering flames to share food and stories with your own tribe. As this month's recipe highlights, there's lots of hearty seasonal fare that can be easily and enjoyably cooked outdoors on an open flame: potatoes in embers, a beef or mushroom stew in an old iron pot, and griddle cakes with sweet spices. The anonymity of the dark and the cosy community of the fireside allows a gentle opportunity for everyone to offer a short story, tall tale or treasured anecdote; perhaps in honour of those we love, that have passed away. Indoors, it's an opportunity to bring out photos of family members, placing them on the mantelpiece, around the hearth or in the kitchen. This season of lost souls and ancestral memories also provides inspiration for making oral history recordings of our elders, relatives or community members, to keep their voices alive. As long as you remember someone, they're never really dead.

12

December

Then hey! for Christmas once a year,
We'll have cakes and ale and beer ...

Gawain and the Green Knight

Christmastime at the court of Camelot: a scene of bright merriment and sea-sonable celebrations, while winter weather rages outside. King Arthur was seated on an oaken chair at the head of the banqueting table, with his knights and their ladies, dressed in their finest attire, seated all around. The happy hum of conversation was occasionally punctuated by the raising of toasts, and the clanking tankards of ale and goblets of wine. A large log fire flamed in the hearth and the hall was hung with branches of evergreen foliage: holly and ivy, mistletoe and yew. From the kitchen drifted sumptuous smells of roasted meats, baked pies, braised vegetables and steamed suet puddings. As the food was being served, King Arthur looked up and saw a little red-breasted robin perched on the window sill. 'Let the poor creature in to feed on the crumbs, for are they not the heralds of good fortune?' He announced to the room.

Just at that moment, the main door of the hall burst open, sending a flurry of snowflakes into the room. There, filling the entire doorframe, was a giant of a man, dressed completely in green with matching green hair. On his head he wore a crown of holly and in his hand was a huge axe with glistening blade. King Arthur warmly welcomed the unexpected guest and invited him to join the table. The Green Knight marched into the middle of the room: 'I'm not here for food, but for sport. Who here, among such knights of fame and legend, will test their mettle against mine?'

Unwilling to break the spell of midwinter merrymaking, none of the knights volunteered. In the end King Arthur was about to stand up himself, when Sir Gawain, the King's youngest nephew, stepped forward instead. 'I am willing to be tested!'

The green giant smiled broadly. 'Very good, then hear my challenge. Take my axe and strike my neck with all your might. If you kill me, my lands and possessions will be yours. However, if I survive you must receive a blow from me in return – at my own dwelling, in a year's time.'

Gawain agreed and gave his word. Then the Green Knight knelt down and bowed his head as Gawain lifted the axe, almost too heavy to hold, and brought it swinging down. The giant's head fell cleanly from its shoulders and rolled onto the stone floor. But then, to the amazement of everyone, the body staggered to its feet and replaced the head on its own shoulders.

'Well struck, Gawain. But as you see, I'm still alive! Seek me in a year's time to fulfil your end of the bargain!'

With that, the Green Knight strode out of the hall, slamming the oak doors behind him.

From that day forward, Gawain was treated like a king among his kinsmen, who were happy to repay his courage with kindness for the rest of the festive season and into the next year. Gawain, caught up in pleasure and pride, gave little more thought to his next meeting with the Green Knight. The seasons kept turning: winter thawed into spring, spring rushed into summer and summer finally faded into autumn. On Michaelmas Day, with the trees turning from green gold, Gawain finally resolved to complete his challenge. Wearing his brightest armour, and riding Arthur's best horse, he set out to find the Green Knight. For the rest of that year, he wandered through the kingdom, heading northwards as winter gradually tightened its icy grip. In late December, on winter solstice itself, he came across a stone castle, in a clearing within a wild woodland. In need of shelter and warmth, Gawain knocked on the door and was immediately welcomed inside by the owner of the castle. That night he was treated as an honoured guest by the lord, and the lady by his side – the most beautiful, beguiling woman Gawain had ever seen.

In the morning he thanked his hosts, telling them he must continue his quest to reach the dwelling of the Green Knight by Christmas Day. The lord laughed loudly and clapped his hands on Gawain's shoulders. 'In that case be at ease, my friend – the place you seek is only half a day's ride and my servant can easily guide you there. Rest here for another three days and recover your strength in the gentle care and company of my wife. I'll be away hunting in the woods by day, but will make a gift to you of anything I catch by nightfall. In return, you must promise to share any favour that you find in my house ...'

Gawain agreed, glad to pause before his impending peril. He rose late the next morning and spent the day conversing by the fireside with the lovely lady of the house. After hours of conversation, she laughed lightly and remarked, 'Never have I been so long in the company of a noble knight who hasn't desired to give me a kiss.'

'Fair lady, I shall not fail where others have obliged,' Gawain replied, leaning forward and kissing her softly on the cheek. That evening the lord returned from his hunting and threw the carcass of a royal stag at Gawain's feet: 'See what I bring for you! Now show me what you have won today.'

Unashamedly, Gawain planted a kiss on his cheek. The same happened the following day – while the lord was out hunting, Gawain enjoyed the company of his lady, this time placing two gentle kisses upon her cheek. That evening, after the hunt, the body of a wild boar was laid out onto the floor. 'We'll eat well tonight!' said the lord. 'What have you gained?' Once more, Gawain diligently delivered the kisses to the lord's own cheek.

For a third day, as the lord was away hunting, Gawain took his fireside ease in the sweet lady's company, finishing with three more delicate kisses. 'You have acted with both grace and restraint,' she said, smiling. 'Please accept this green girdle as a gift from me. It has little value, as such, yet much virtue. Anyone who wears this ribbon cannot be slain by arrow or sword or axe.'

That evening, when the lord returned, he threw a severed fox's tail on the floor, drops of red staining the grey stone floor. Gawain stepped forward to return the three kisses he had gained, but not the green ribbon. That night they feasted until late, with fine food and flagons of blood-red wine. Much mirth was made between the three of them. The next day, fear rising in his chest for the first time, Gawain took his leave. Led by a servant, he rode through the forest and down a deep valley to the entrance of a craggy cave. There he saw the Green Knight slowly sharpening his axe against a granite boulder.

'Ha! I'm glad to see at least one knight in Arthur's England is willing to keep his word and repay his debts! Now take your stance, as I take my chance ...'

Gawain knelt before the Green Knight. But as the axe came swinging down, Gawain heard the sound of a wren's alarm call. His head flinched sideways slightly and the blade missed its mark. 'You moved – I'm owed another blow,' bellowed the Green Knight.

This time, the wren flew down right beside Gawain, who instinctively turned his head as the axe was falling, so once more the blade found only thin air. 'Be still this time, or it will be worse for you!'

Remembering the lady's green girdle, hidden within his outer garments, Gawain stood firm. The axe came down and this time Gawain did not flinch, yet still the blade only grazed the nape of his neck; raising a few beads of blood.

'Rise up, Sir Gawain, the challenge is over! You have kept your head because you kept your promise and faithfully returned my lady's affection. See now: I am the same man as the lord of the castle. However, because you kept the green girdle from me, these few drops of blood were your payment. Now go home, a free man, with your honour and my friendship ...'

Gawain took the long way home, enjoying the countryside through its changing mantle of seasons, finally arriving at Camelot at Christmastime – with a stirring story to tell.

Midwinter Magic

Winter solstice – usually occurring on either 21st or 22nd December – is the darkest point of the year, when the Earth's Northern Hemisphere is tilted farthest away from the sun. But that celestial nadir is also the magical moment when the solar year is reset. After the solstice, the light gradually begins to grow again and the cycle of the seasons is renewed. Many ancient archaeological sites, including Stonehenge in England and Newgrange in Ireland, were constructed to mark the position of the sun at winter solstice – to hold the sacredness of the moment when the sun is both killed and rekindled. The Romans referred to this date as Sol Invictus – the Unconquered Sun – celebrating its annual resurrection as the universal provider of light and life. Similarly, winter solstice was known as Modranicht in Anglo-Saxon, meaning 'Mother's Night' and marking the rebirth of the solar year.

Many seasonal stories and traditions at this time of year incorporate the narrative theme of death and resurrection, including the Arthurian legend of Gawain and the Green Knight, where a mysterious midwinter guest performs a miraculous feat of reincarnation. The Green Knight, with evergreen skin and holly crown, resonates strongly with the Holly King from Celtic mythology: an archetypal deity that rules during the waning half of the year, from midsummer to midwinter, who we first encountered in June. At this point in the seasonal cycle the royal mantle is passed to the Oak King, who reigns during the growing half of the year; perhaps embodied in the story by Sir Gawain himself, with his heart of oak and strength of spirit. An alternative Old English name for December was 'oak month', thought to honour the visible virtues of oak trees – standing strong in withstanding winter's weather.

Yule Be Merry and Bright

By midwinter the nights are at their longest, nearly nine hours longer than midsummer. In this cold, dark and dreary time of the year there has long been a strong, shared need to brighten our homes with food, fire and good company. The Romans celebrated Saturnalia for several days around 17th December, in honour of the eponymous god of agriculture. It's a riotous affair that introduced many familiar festive elements into later Christmas celebrations: drinking and dancing; presents and party games. One distinctive element of Saturnalia was the temporary inversion of the social order: slaves were served by their masters, the poor were provided with plenty and children gave orders to the adults. Sometimes a representative ruler was elected as the Lord of Misrule, often through hiding a dried bean in a cake. Just as gallant Gawain, the young nephew of King Arthur, was elevated to king-for-a-year before he eventually sets out to face the fearsome Green Knight.

Yule, originating from Old Norse, designates a three-day midwinter festival celebrating the wheel of the year reaching its simultaneous culmination and reinitiation. The Anglo-Saxon names for full moons in December and January are simply Moon Before Yule and Moon After Yule; highlighting the cultural importance of such celebrations. Festive fires, bright lights, music and merriment were all used to woo the new-born infant sun to grow in light and warmth. It also gave rise to the custom of Yule Logs: long pieces of timber ceremonially burnt in the hearth on Christmas Eve, through to Christmas morning, in order to invoke good fortune and prosperity. If the Yule Log burns well, then so too will the sun shine brightly in the year ahead. In the past, there was often spirited competition between communities for the biggest Yule Log, which sometimes needed to be dragged by horses. In a few West Country pubs, where the tradition continues, Yule Logs are generally fashioned from a bundle of ashen faggots bound together with strips of bark. At every bursting of a bark-band in the fireplace, a toast is proposed, and glasses filled – generally resulting in a very merry Christmas! Traditionally, the cold ashes from Yule fires are sprinkled around the house for protection and across the farm to invoke fertility. A splinter of wood should also be reserved to light the following year's Yule Log.

> Come by with a noise,
> My merry, merry boys
> The Christmas log for the firing ...

Festive feasts are a common element of Yuletide, Saturnalia and Christmas celebrations. It's a time when, for once, moderation is gleefully forsaken and plenty is both provided for and praised. Rich, luxurious foods – roast meats, pastry pies and sweet, sticky cakes – appear on the table to grace the occasion; including the ultimate comfort food of Christmas pudding itself. One day was clearly not enough for such much-needed and long-anticipated midwinter merrymaking. Yule was at least three days, Saturnalia lasted a week, Christmas has its twelve days. In medieval times the festivities continued, on and off, all the way through to Candlemas (2nd February).

> A many mince pies as you taste at Christmas,
> As many happy months as you will have ...

Flavour of the Month

Thirteen x Thirteen-Ingredient Mince Pies

During Shakespeare's era, supposedly, the fashion was to make mince pies not only with minced lamb, but thirteen different ingredients; no more, no fewer. We took on the thirteen-ingredient mince pie challenge, which has produced an extraordinarily tasty result.

We use a lot of natural animal fats in our restaurant – suet, lard and tallow. Grass-reared animal fats are a valuable source of omega-3 fatty acids, so here's an opportunity here to get some of those nutrients into our mince pies. We omit lamb mince in this recipe, given that tastes have changed today, but don't skimp on the fat – it's good for bones and brains!

We often freeze cawl fat – the white, crumbly fat stored around the chest cavity of grass-eating animals. Ask your butcher for some; they will gladly oblige. The best alcohol to fortify these saffron-tinged pastry pies is Pedro Ximénez sherry; it expands the dried fruit tones admirably and moistens the mincemeat to a dream.

MINCEMEAT
Makes 800g

> 300g Bramley apples, peeled and finely cubed
> 100g Medjool dates, stones removed
> 200g currants
> 100g fresh beef suet, grated finely from frozen
> 100g light muscovado
> ½ teaspoon black pepper
> ½ teaspoon mace
> ½ teaspoon cinnamon
> 100ml Pedro Ximénez sherry

Cook the cubed apple, currants and sherry together for thirteen minutes. Squish the dates to a pulp and add to the pan with the remaining ingredients. Bring to a simmer once more, making sure the sugar has cooked out. Add more sherry should you desire, as it carries extra sweetness. Place in two 400g sterilised jars while hot, attach lids and let cool before storing in a dark cupboard.

PASTRY

    375g plain flour
    250g salted butter, softened
    125g light muscovado sugar
    Two pinches of saffron dissolved in ⅓ cup water
    One medium free-range egg, beaten
    Preheat oven to 190°C

- In a mixing bowl, sift in the plain flour and make a well for the beaten egg.
- Add the sugar and butter and rub the ingredients together, loosening with a dash of saffron water to make a dough. Be mindful not to overwork the dough. Wrap and place in the fridge for thirteen minutes.
- Roll out the pastry on a floured surface to 3mm thick and cut into twelve rounds using a 9cm cutting ring to line a twelve-hole muffin tray, followed by twelve lids cut using an 8cm fluted pastry cutter. Re-roll the leftover pieces of pastry to hand raise the thirteenth mince pie case – lucky for someone!
- Divide the mincemeat between the pies, filling them to about three quarters full.
- Bake for twenty-two to twenty-four minutes, then cool on wire racks.
- Enjoy this Christmas champion with family, good-quality brandy and Lancashire cheese.

'Deck the Halls with Boughs of Holly'

One of the longest-observed midwinter traditions is the gathering and bringing in of evergreen vegetation: holly and ivy, mistletoe and yew. Sprays of winter greenery provide a vivid symbol of the perennial nature of life, as well as a reminder that the season of growth will come round again. They also serve to decorate the household with brightness at an otherwise drab time of year, especially boughs with colourful berries; precursors, perhaps, to modern-day fairy lights. Holly's Christmas credentials are enhanced through its association with Saturn (and therefore Saturnalia) and the sharp spikes and blood-red berries are seen as symbolic of Jesus's crown of thorns, as portrayed in the famous carol: 'The Holly and the Ivy'. Traditionally, the plant is only ever cut at this time of year, when it serves as both winter fodder for livestock and protection against malevolent magic. Evergreen wreaths hung on doors in December are also seen as a representation of the wheel of the year, as it turns full circle.

Christmas trees continue the tradition of bringing evergreen vegetation indoors. They reportedly originated in Germany and were famously popularised in Britain by Queen Victoria and Prince Albert. Lit candles placed on the dark green branches (now mostly replaced by artificial lights) add to the symbolic hopefulness of renewed light, as well as life, in the dead of winter. Mistletoe, with olive green leaves and glistening white berries, also has mythic potency at this time of year. It is a symbol of virility, as reflected in the custom of kissing under the mistletoe. In Norse myth, Baldur the Bright was killed by Loki, the god of mischief, using an arrow made from mistletoe. His mother wept tears of sorrow that formed the plant's clouded crystal berries. The mistle thrush is named after its fondness for eating mistletoe and can often be heard singing loudly at midwinter, even in wild weather, giving rise to its other folk name of stormcock.

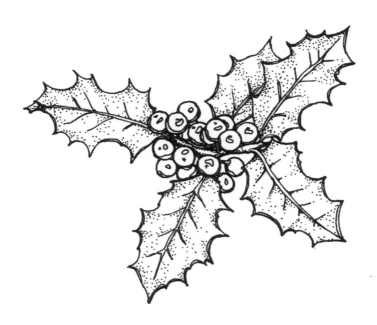

Robin Goodfellow

The robin and the wren, God Almighty's cock and hen.
Kill a robin or a wren, never prosper boys or men.

The chorus of birdsong has dwindled by December, leaving the plaintive notes of thrushes, robins and wrens; loud but lonesome. With their faithful carolling and chirpy nature throughout winter, robins in particular are held in fond affection at Christmas; as reflected in Christmas card imagery. In folklore, robins are held as harbingers of good luck and are believed to grant wishes at midwinter, therefore, they should never be chased away. They also feature symbolically as good spirits of the orchard during wassailing ceremonies (see January). A Christian legend tells that the robin's breast feathers were stained red by Jesus's blood, when trying to remove the crown of thorns. Another, older, midwinter myth holds a different explanation for those fiery red feathers …

Wren and Robin Bring Fire

In the beginning, there was no fire. Humans, without fur or feathers, suffered terribly in the cold of winter and the long nights were miserably dark. But little Wren, while travelling through the underworld, had found fire in the depths of hell and was determined to bring it back to the world. The brave bird flew through twisting subterranean tunnels, searching the deepest caves and darkest holes, getting hotter the deeper she went. Eventually, she reached Hell's inferno and deftly darted down to grab a burning coal. Back she flew, as quick as her wings could carry her, but the smouldering cinder ignited her tail feathers. As she emerged in flames from the cave, Robin bravely and impulsively wrapped his wings around her. In doing so, he managed to suffocate the flames with his own chest feathers. Then, using the burning ember, they kindled a flickering fire with straw and twigs. Since then, wrens have short, stubby tails, robins have bright, red breasts, and we have fire to keep us warm in winter.

The Cutty Wren

The wren's Latin name – *Troglodytes* – means 'cave dweller' and they can often be seen emerging from dark holes among the undergrowth in the depth of winter. Like robins, they have strong cultural significance in Britain and Ireland, featuring in many folk tales and folksongs. In one well-known myth, all birds gather together to choose a king through a flying competition. Despite the physical supremacy of the eagle over the other birds, clever wren manages to win the race by hanging onto his tail feathers. Eagle disputed the result, of course, but little wren still loudly proclaims her royal pedigree from every hedgerow. It's been suggested this ancient legend might also reflect a moment in Britain's military history: the wren was an emblem of Celtic tribes and the eagle a symbol of the Roman empire.

> The wren, the wren, the king of all birds,
> On St Stephen's Day was caught in the furze.

Despite being held in high esteem, an old folk song called 'The Cutty Wren' (cutty refers to their cut-short tails), holds a narrative of the ceremonial sacrifice of the wren as the King of Birds. It's also the basis of a traditional midwinter custom called Hunting the Wren, once widely held on St Stephen's Day (26th December), which still continues in some places in Ireland and the Isle of Man every year. Thankfully, it's ritualistic rather than realistic these days: a group of young men, known as 'wren boys', parade around the local neighbourhood dressed in costumes, singing songs, with a figurative wren held aloft on a stick. Symbolically, it's yet another tradition that seems to honour the midwinter myth of the perennial death and revival of the sun.

Christmas Champions

> In comes I, Old Father Christmas!
> Welcome in or welcome not,
> I hope Old Father Christmas
> Will never be forgot!

Mummers' plays, as a folk tradition with plentiful local variations, are performed at various seasonally sensitive times of year, including Easter,

St George's Day and All Souls. At Christmas and New Year, however, they come into their own, echoing the riotousness of Saturnalia and continuing the merrymaking of medieval festivities. In essence, they are rough and ready ritualised performances, delightfully unencumbered by narrative subtlety or acting ability. Lack of finesse, however, is amply compensated by a colourful cast of costumed characters, frequently reflecting local history and geography. Traditionally, they begin with an initial character (often Old Father Christmas at this time of year) begging the attention of the audience, the proceeding as each individual player takes a turn to speak in rhyming couplets. The players invariably receive plentiful food and (especially) drink in exchange for performing at pubs and other venues around the local area; sometimes totalling half a dozen before the night is out. In the past, mummers' plays would have provided an opportunity for supplementing meagre incomes. The word 'mummers' itself is said to derive from the ragged disguises, which allowed low-paid labourers to effectively beg for money without being recognised.

Although largely medieval in origin rather than pagan, they nevertheless reflect enduring themes around the cycling of the seasons. In particular, the ostentatious killing and miraculous resurrection of one or more of the key characters (typically the most vainglorious) is seen by some as a representation of the death of the old year and the rebirth of the new. Some mummers' plays, such as the Marshfield Paper Boys who perform every Boxing Day in that village, have a respectably long tradition. Many more have been enthusiastically revived and/or reinvented in recent times around the UK. As such they provide a welcome opportunity for locally distinctive, seasonally relevant community celebrations, full of festive spirit, but devoid of overtly religious beliefs or commercial trappings.

Grey Mare

In Wales and its borderlands, the Mari Lwyd rides out at Christmas and New Year; a custom somewhere between mummers' plays and wassailing (see January). Comprising, in physical form, a bleached horse's skull on a pole with a white cloth covering, the Mari Lwyd ceremonially visits local pubs and households, along with a colourful and noisy entourage of attendants. On arrival the troop beg entry, through a traditional song in Welsh, which is then followed by a lively (and sometimes lengthy) debate with the host of the house in ribald rhymes. Once gaining admittance, the revellers bring good cheer in exchange for ample beer, as the Mari Lwyd continues to canter around causing

playful mischief. As with many other living traditions, it has widely been revived across Wales in recent times. The meaning of Mari Lwyd is uncertain, but is sometimes translated as Grey Mare. Allegedly, this reflects a grey mare that was either ridden by the Virgin Mary, or kicked out of the stable to make room for the Holy Family at Jesus's birth.

Child's Play

From sun god to God's son, midwinter is the season that celebrates divine birth. It continues to hold a long-standing cultural indulgence towards children at Christmastime. On the day after Saturnalia there was a Roman festival called Juvenalia – with feasts and presents for the young. The child friendliness is bolstered by St Nicholas, the patron saint of both boys and girls. His feast day is earlier in the month (6th December), but his legendary deeds in helping the needy and leaving gifts for the poor have helped shape the familiar figure of Santa Claus, who appears annually, with the tinkling of sleigh bells, on Christmas Eve. In England, the tradition of anointing a chorister as Boy Bishop over the festive period (normally Holy Innocents on 28th December) was once widespread among cathedral cities. It still takes place at Hereford, where he leads processions, takes the collection and even preaches the sermon.

Elf Service

Once upon a time, every home had its own 'house elf' – a supernatural creature – that protected the property from harm. In England these were commonly called hobgoblins (or hobs), in Scotland brownies and in Scandinavia gnomes. They are the spirits of home and hearth, making sure everything is looked after in the household, as well as the stables and barns, without being seen. They are also famously highly sensitive creatures, however, and woe betide those who wilfully choose to neglect or disrespect them. One such cautionary tale concerns a girl who selfishly ate the sweetened porridge left out for the house elf on Christmas Eve and was then magically compelled to spend the whole night dancing with the hob until she collapsed of exhaustion in the morning.

Several festive customs that are nowadays associated with Father Christmas, seem to derive from folklore about the house elf. Traditionally, they come and go from the house via the chimney, and often leave helpful gifts by the hearth. In contrast to current Christmas consumerism, perhaps, they only ever give to those in need, and no more than is needed. In return, especially at this time of year, they expect token offerings of food and drink, in gratitude for the blessings they bring to the household. As Father Christmas himself knows: a glass of whisky and a buttery biscuit always go down well. In particular, these household sprites are said to keep watch over domestic livestock during the long, cold nights of midwinter.

The Christmas Cabin

Early one morning, on a cold December's day, a mysterious cloth bundle was left at the doorstep of a little cottage in rural Ireland. The couple who lived there were greatly surprised to discover that the package contained a baby girl – alive and well, but clearly abandoned. Despite being poor, with several children of their own, they accepted her into their home as one of their own; naming her Oona. The girl grew up happy and healthy within the only family she ever knew. Eventually, the old couple passed away, leaving their cottage to the eldest son and his own young family. Oona now had to leave the house and make her own way in the world.

She travelled for a few days, carrying a bundle of belongings on her back, which included an embroidered tablecloth that her mother had left her. Before long, she found work in the house of another family – cooking, cleaning and looking after their children in exchange for a place to live. After several years, when the children were old enough to fend for themselves, she moved on to another household. So, the pattern of Oona's simple, selfless life story was laid out. Each time she moved, from one home to another, she left behind her own warmth and kindness and the bundle on her back got a little bigger. The older she got, however, the more she longed for a little place of her own.

One year, she found herself between work, walking for weeks without finding anywhere to stay. By late December, flurries of snowflakes began to fall from the grey sky and she worried that she might freeze to death out in the open. It was just then that she heard a strange merry music carried on the blustery breeze and, peering through the blizzard, she saw a group of small figures, dancing lightly on the freshly fallen snow. Summoning all of her courage, Oona approached the throng of Little People and politely asked if they knew of any place to take shelter. A ripple of laughter filled the air, before one of them answered, 'Of course we do, Oona! Put your foot on mine and see your own cabin, warm and welcoming.'

Amazed by what she heard, Oona nevertheless did as she was bid, very gently resting the tip of her shoe on the tiny foot of the fairy. Instantly, a veil was lifted from her eyes. Just a few feet away was a little wooden cabin, with yellow light pouring out of the window and open doorway. Stepping inside, she found a fire roaring in the hearth, a bed covered with warm woollen blankets and a table set with two chairs. It was everything she'd ever dreamed of – a little place of her own! Untying her much-travelled bundle, she lovingly spread her mother's embroidered cloth across the table; her old eyes shining with tears. The next day, Christmas Eve, a weary traveller came knocking at the door – surprised to find a homely cabin in the middle of nowhere. Oona gave him a warm welcome and together they ate a fine festive feast, magically provided by her mysterious benefactors.

Oona lived happily in the cabin for the rest of her life and received many guests over the years, especially at midwinter. But, strange to say, each visitor reported that the Christmas cabin was situated in a different place in Ireland. Oona herself never saw the fairy folk again, but she always remembered to leave a little something by the fireplace, especially on Christmas Eve.

Old Roots, New Shoots

TREE DRESSING

If the sun shines through the trees on Christmas Day,
At autumn time, lots of fruits they'll display.

Decorating a living tree is a festive custom with deep roots. Many countries around the world have ceremonies and celebrations that honour the ecological and cultural importance of particular trees by ornamenting their branches. Tree Dressing Day, as an official annual tradition, was initiated by Common Ground in 1990 (the same year as October's Apple Day) to help acknowledge both the global importance and local significance of trees. While not as widely established as its autumn sibling, many winter tree dressing celebrations still take place each year on, or around, the first weekend in December. The focus is often a locally distinctive tree, upstanding within the community, which is gleefully given the royal treatment: covered with coloured ribbons and fancy garlands, hung with twinkling lights and warmly toasted with song, story and merriment.

In contrast to bringing a Christmas tree indoors to 're-nature' our homes, tree dressing involves going outdoors to celebrate trees in *their* place; and in turn helping us to appreciate our own local places. December is also a magical time to go for a wild winter walk, to see trees in their naked glory – standing steadfast and strong against cold, clear skies. Where appropriate, you might also take the opportunity to search for your own Yule Log to burn at home and bring bright blessings on the just-dawning New Year.

So the seasons have sung their year-long cycle of songs. And, in the end, we're back to the beginning …

A Note on Songs

Roud folk song index numbers have been listed where applicable.

Sources

Adams, R. & Hooper, M., *Nature Through the Seasons* (Harmondsworth: Penguin, 1976).

Alexander, M., *A Companion to the Folklore, Myths & Customs of Britain* (Stroud: Sutton Publishing, 2002).

Anon, *Folk-Lore & Legends of England* (London: EP Publishing, 1972).

Anon, *Folklore, Myths and Legends of Britain* (London: Reader's Digest, 1973).

Anon, *Scottish Fairy Tales* (Edinburgh: Lomond Books, 1998).

Arrowsmith, N. with Moorse, G., *A Field Guide to the Little People* (London: Macmillan, 1977).

Baker, M., *Folklore and Customs of Rural England* (Newton Abbot: Readers Union, 1975).

Baker, M., *The Gardener's Folklore* (North Vancouver: David & Charles, 1977).

Baker, M., *Discovering the Folklore of Plants* (Princes Risborough: Shire publications, 2001).

Binney, R., *Nature's Ways: Lore, Legend, Fact and Fiction* (Cincinnati: David & Charles, 2006).

Briggs, K., *A Dictionary of British Folk-Tales* (London: Routledge & Kegan Paul, 1970).

Briggs, K., *A Dictionary of Fairies* (Harmondsworth: Penguin, 1977).

Briggs, K., & Tongue, R. *Folktales of England* (Chicago: The University of Chicago Press, 1965).

Cooper, Q. & Sullivan, P., *Maypoles, Martyrs and Mayhem: 366 Days of British Myths, Customs and Eccentricities* (London: Bloomsbury, 1994).

Copper, B., *A Song for Every Season: A Hundred Years of a Sussex Farming Family* (Newton Abbot: Country Book Club, 1972).

Crossley-Holland, K., *The Old Stories: Folk Tales from East Anglia and the Fen Country* (Cambridge: Colt Books, 1997).

Clifford, C. & King A., *England in Particular: A Celebration of the Commonplace, the Local, the Vernacular and the Distinctive* (London: Hodder & Stoughton, 2006).

Deas, L., *Flower Favourites* (London: George Allen, 1898).

Grigson, G., *The Englishman's Flora* (Oxford: Helicon, 1996).

Grimm, J. & W., *Complete Fairy Tales* (London: Routledge & Kegan Paul, 1948).

Groom, N., *The Seasons: An Elegy for the Passing Year* (London: Atlantic Books, 2013).

Froud, B. & Lee, A., *Faeries* (New York: Harry N. Abrams, 1978).

Hole, C., *English Traditional Customs* (London: Batsford, 1975).

Hageneder, F., *The Spirit of the Trees: Science, Symbiosis and Inspiration* (New York: Continuum, 2001).

Hole, C., *British Folk Customs* (London: Book Club Associates, 1976).

Hutton, R., *The Stations of the Sun: A History of the Ritual Year in Britain* (New York: Oxford University Press, 1997).

Kindred, G., *Earth Wisdom: A Heartwarming Mixture of the Spiritual, the Practical and the Proactive* (London: Hay House, 2004).

Leighton, C., *The Farmer's Year: A Calendar of English Husbandry* (Dorset: Little Toller books, 2018).

Macdonald, M.R., *Earth Care: World Folktales to Talk About* (Connecticut: Linnet Books, 1999).

Macpherson, G.W., *Highland Myths and Legends* (Croydon: Bookmarque, 2005).

Manning-Sanders, R., (ed.) *Festivals* (London: Heinemann, 1972).

Marshall, S., *Everyman's Book of English Folk Tales* (Guernsey: Guernsey Press, 1981).

Montley, P., *In Nature's Honour: Myths and Rituals Celebrating the Earth* (Boston: Skinner House Books, 2005).

Newland, R., *Dark Dorset Calendar Customs* (Bideford, CFZ Press, 2007).

Paterson, J.M., *Tree Wisdom: The Definitive Guide Book to the Myth, Folklore and Healing Power of Trees* (London: Element, 1996).

Philip, N., *The Penguin Book of English Folktales* (London: Penguin, 1992).

Riordan, J., *Folk-Tales of the British Isles* (Moscow: Raduga, 1987).

Roud, S., *The English Year* (London: Penguin Books, 2006).

Roud, S. & Bishop, J. (eds), *The New Penguin Book of English Folk-Songs* (London: Penguin, 2012).

Sawyer, R., *The Wee Christmas Cabin of Carn-na-ween* (Massachusetts: Candlewick Press, 2005).

Smith, G.I., *Folk Tales of the Highlands*. (London: Thomas Nelson & Sons, 1953).

Stevenson, P., *Welsh Folk Tales* (Stroud: The History Press, 2017).

St. Leger-Gordon, R., *The Witchcraft and Folklore of Dartmoor* (Newton Abbot: Peninsula Press, 1996).

Siddons Heginworth, I., *Environmental Arts Therapy and the Tree of Life* (Exeter: Spirit's Rest, 2009).

Watson, E.L. & Tunnicliffe, R.A., *What to Look for in Winter* (Loughborough: Ladybird Books, 1959).

Watson, E.L. & Tunnicliffe, R.A., *What to Look for in Autumn* (Loughborough: Ladybird Books, 1960).

Watson, E.L. & Tunnicliffe, R.A., *What to Look for in Summer* (Loughborough: Ladybird Books, 1960).

Watson, E.L. & Tunnicliffe, R.A., *What to Look for in Spring* (Loughborough: Ladybird Books, 1961).

Westwood, J. & Simpson, J., *The Lore of the Land: A Guide to England's Legends* (London: Penguin, 2005).

Williamson, D. with Williamson, L., *Fireside Tales of the Traveller Children* (Edinburgh: Birlinn, 2009).

Williamson, D., *The Flight of the Golden Bird* (Glasgow: Floris Books, 2013).

Wright, J., *The Forager's Calendar* (London: Profile Books, 2019).

Common Ground

Common Ground is a charity based in Dorset, which has been at the forefront of community conservation and environmental education in England
for the last forty years. We are a small, grassroots organisation that aims to
reconnect people with nature and inspire communities to become engaged
with, and responsible for, their local environment. We believe that celebrating the particular places where you live, and enjoying the wildlife and
landscape on your doorstep, through the changing seasons, is at the heart of
meaningful conservation.

Common Ground was founded in 1983 by Sue Clifford, Angela King and
the late writer Roger Deakin, with the idea of such 'Local Distinctiveness' at
its core. The name carried a nod to Richard Mabey's influential book of the
time, *The Common Ground*. It encapsulates the view that environmentalism
is a concern common to all of us, and that it might be about the ordinary
and the close-to-home as much as about the rare and exceptional. Since then
projects like Apple Day, New Milestones, Parish Maps, Tree Dressing and
Community Woodlands have captured the imagination of hundreds of communities all over the country and stimulated the growth of myriad locally
maintained offshoots.

Today, under the directorship of Adrian Cooper, we continue to connect
people with their own common ground through music, art exhibitions,
film-making, publishing, events and education. Current projects, such as
Seasonal Schools, Arboreal, Trees and Woods Almanac, Exeter Tree Tales
and LEAF!, are helping communities to make meaningful, long-lasting
connections with their local environment. In particular, Common Ground
are developing various endeavours that actively celebrate the cultural value

of the seasons and exploring how seasonality can become part of our ever-busy twenty-first-century lives. We believe that celebrating the seasons and forming attachments to place are essential to our identity and can empower communities to express themselves and take action in resourceful, imaginative and inclusive ways.

www.commonground.org.uk

Matthew Pennington
The Ethicurean

Matthew is co-founder of The Ethicurean restaurant at Barley Wood Walled Garden, North Somerset, and a published food writer. Celebrating two decades of exploration within the UK culinary scene, his interests combine cookery, native produce, wild food, fermentation, regenerative agriculture, soil health, mycology and food folklore. As a writer, he believes every possible subject can be comprehended from within the kitchen and garden, and with irrepressible curiosity is attempting to do just that.

Over the last decade, Matthew and Martin have collaborated on numerous legendary seasonal celebrations, spanning St Georges' Day to summer solstice and Apple Day to midwinter wassailing. Each event comprises a specially curated menu of stories and food for guests and diners to enjoy, as well as highlighting the importance of seasonality, sustainability and provenance. Matthew is thrilled to share some of his philosophy and techniques through the bespoke recipes within *Telling the Seasons*.

www.theethicurean.com

Society *for* **Storytelling**

Since 1993, The Society for Storytelling has championed the ancient art of oral storytelling and its long and honourable history – not just as entertainment, but also in education, health, and inspiring and changing lives. Storytellers, enthusiasts and academics support and are supported by this registered charity to ensure the art is nurtured and developed throughout the UK.

Many activities of the Society are available to all, such as locating storytellers on the Society website, taking part in our annual National Storytelling Week at the start of every February, purchasing our quarterly magazine Storylines, or attending our Annual Gathering – a chance to revel in engaging performances, inspiring workshops, and the company of like-minded people.

You can also become a member of the Society to support the work we do. In return, you receive free access to Storylines, discounted tickets to the Annual Gathering and other storytelling events, the opportunity to join our mentorship scheme for new storytellers, and more. Among our great deals for members is a 30% discount off titles from The History Press.

For more information, including how to join, please visit

www.sfs.org.uk